GODS OF THRONES

A PILGRIM'S GUIDE TO THE
RELIGIONS OF ICE AND FIRE

VOL.1

A.RON HUBBARD   ANTHONY LE DONNE

"Bursting with insight and full of japes, this book will teach you much and more. *Gods of Thrones* will deepen your experience of the novels and remind you why you loved them in the first place. Clearly, these guys drink and know things."

— CHAD CARMICHAEL, PHD
Professor of Philosophy
Indiana University–Purdue University, Indianapolis

"*Gods of Thrones* presents an overview of the religions and belief systems of HBO's *Game of Thrones* television series and the book series that inspired it, George R. R. Martin's *A Song of Ice and Fire*. A.Ron Hubbard and Anthony Le Donne skillfully weave humor, history, pop culture, comparative religion, and their expansive knowledge of the series into a rich, engaging tapestry that even Cersei Lannister wouldn't dare to part with. *Gods of Thrones* has it all—from the gods of ice to those of fire and from Celtic-inspired traditions of The North and the First Man, to the Catholic-inspired Faith of the Seven of the South and the Andal invaders. The authors also pay homage to several fan theories from the books and show (e.g., "Is Roose Bolton a vampire?"). Best of all, they write for both show and book audiences; both will find something of interest in *Gods of Thrones*. This work is a must-read for fans of the show or the book series who are looking to learn more about the religions in the series—or a good laugh. Indeed, I wish I had had *Gods of Thrones* available as a companion book when teaching my *A Game of Thrones* course last year."

— GREGORY D. WEBSTER, PHD
Professor of Psychology
University of Florida

"True to form, A.Ron and Anthony blend entertaining wit with their significant real-world and in-universe knowledge to produce a remarkably enjoyable tour through the religions of *Game of Thrones*."

— JIM JONES
Cohost, Bald Move

Original illustrations by Chase Stone.
Graphic design by Steve Gentile.

GODS

OF

THRONES

And behold! Towards us coming in a boat
An old man, hoary with the hair of eld,
Crying, Woe unto you, ye souls depraved!
Hope nevermore to look upon the heavens;
I come to guide you to the other shore,
To the eternal shades in fire and ice.
                                    —DANTE ALIGHIERI

Volume 1

Hi, I'm A.RON, cohost of Bald Move's creatively titled podcast, "The *Game of Thrones* Podcast by Bald Move." On November 9, 2017, a guy named "Anthony" sent a message to Bald Move's general *Game of Thrones* email inbox. My cohost Jim and I were just finishing up the rewatch of season 2—which means at that point we had been talking about *Game of Thrones* nonstop for about eighteen weeks. I was already looking forward to the holiday season and taking a few weeks off at the end of the year to enjoy Christmas and the New Year with my family.

Now, I get *a lot* of email during *Game of Thrones* season. Way too much to possibly read on air, and on some weeks too much to read in any kind of detail at all. I've become pretty good at sizing up an email based on its size, introduction, and general composition, and can often tell at a glance whether an email is going to make it into the podcast.

This email was different; it was led by the words "***not for airtime***" at the top. *Not for airtime?* Nobody starts off an email like that. You send emails to our *Game of Thrones* inbox *precisely because* you're hoping to run the gauntlet and rise above the hundreds, if not thousands of other people sending feedback to get read on air.

What Anthony wanted—as you can now see—was to collaborate on a book. He was meeting with publishers to pitch some ideas he was kicking around. One of them was a "chapter-by-chapter treatment of the various religions, beliefs, and systems of praxis in the world of ice and fire." Who was this guy who throws around words like *praxis*?

Well, Anthony is a religious scholar; he's thought a lot about ancient religions and how they intersect with cultures and peoples, and how that process gives rise to new religions and reformations, which in turn merge and meld and fragment and decline. I could immediately see the appeal of this kind of thinking applied to the world of *Game of Thrones*.

As a huge fan of George Martin's *A Song of Ice and Fire,* I'm always hungry for new ways to think about the material, new lenses from which to view it, and new ideas and theories that spark discussion and add new layers of appreciation for our favorite characters. A few days later, I responded to Anthony's email that I was interested. After much persistent and yet patient prodding (it must be said Anthony is very good at wrangling a very busy and easily distracted podcaster), we came to terms in early January 2018 to cowrite the book you now hold in your hands.

The idea is to take his scholarship and background in comparative religion and wed it to my knowledge of *Game of Thrones* lore and general irreverence that I've acquired from eight years of professional podcasting and a lifetime of being a smartass. I've always had a weakness for serious scholarship in the pursuit of the minimally important or even the absurd. From Larry Niven writing about Superman's love life (*Man of Steel, Woman of Kleenex,* 1969) to astrophysicist Curtis Saxon contemplating the inevitable Ewok holocaust after exhaustively calculating the Death Star's energy output (on the order of 1,000,000,000,000,000,000,000,000,000,000 watts, in case you were wondering), we are hoping to tap into this long history of entertaining analysis of pop culture using the full battery of intellectual weaponry.

We both learned many things and laughed a lot while making this book. Anthony and I hope that, whether you're an initiate or a maester yourself, you'll pick up some new and intriguing ideas and have fun doing so.

A.RON HUBBARD

Cincinnati, Ohio

Contents

GoT Religion?

HOW GEORGE GOT RELIGION

A SONG OF ICE AND FIRE IS A BIT LIKE COUNTY LOCKUP. You might get religion or you might get a shiv in your kidney. These options, mind you, are not mutually exclusive. George R. R. Martin's world—like the real world—is a mess of entanglements. You've got messianic agnostics, pious scoundrels, calculating zealots, and religious reformers. To play the *Game of Thrones* you've got to master the rules of religious politics.

Modern folk—including most HBO viewers—make a general distinction between sacred and secular. It's just the cultural reality of the modern Western mind. The American mantra "separation of church and state" is a case in point. But for most of human history, a separation of church and state was unimaginable. And here, little lord, is where George R. R. Martin comes at you hard and heavy. Are you ready for him? *We think that you're not!* Martin eats, breathes, and sweats political intrigue. And because his political plots are premodern, they are infused with religion (or what we would now call religion).

For all of his adorable quirks, Martin is rotten with history. His canvas is high fantasy, but he paints with ancient perspectives, medieval plots, and famous personalities. If you look closely enough, you'll find a spectrum of literary echoes ranging from Cleopatra (Ptolemaic Egypt) to Clarence Clemons (E Street Band). Martin knows that a medieval-based fiction—if it's going to pass the authenticity smell test—must be saturated with the sacred.

Martin, in his own words, is keenly "interested in the people of history. There are so many wonderful stories among wars and battles and seductions and betrayals and the choices that people make; so many things that you would be hard-pressed to make up." He continues, "And then, of course, I don't make it up, but I take it and I file off the serial numbers and I turn it up to eleven, and I change the color from red to purple and I have a great incident for the books."[1]

There is no doubt, for example, that Tyrion's plotline is based (in part) on the rumors and theologies orbiting Richard III. Martin has taken the history of Richard III and exploited the rumors of Richard's deformities. Then he places Tyrion in a plotline with a few other characters who smell like War of the Roses types. But he turns the story upside down so that you can't predict Tyrion's outcome. In a sense, Martin borrows from history for a texture of realism but changes enough of the major features of these stories to make them original. In other words, his stories "file off the serial numbers."

In talking about Tyrion's similarities with Richard, Martin says that Tyrion is "hated by the gods, so they twisted his body into unfortunate shapes. This is a clear sign of the evil inside him. This is how the medieval mindset worked." But, of course, Richard wasn't really deformed, and Martin knows this. "He wasn't a hunchback. He didn't have a twisted arm.... The Tudor historians tried to make him a physically twisted, deceitful, kinslaying, child-slaying monster. And a lot of what happened to Richard III is happening to Tyrion."[2]

This tells us something important about Martin's worldbuilding: *he's just as interested in the rumors of*

1. "Real History behind Game of Thrones (Explained by Historians & George R. R. Martin)," YouTube video, 40:14, published July 14, 2016.

2. "Real History," YouTube, July 14, 2016. We deal with Tyrion and Richard III more in our chapter titled "The Faithless and the Hound."

history as he is by the facts. Sometimes it's the rumors, the legends, and the superstitions that reveal how the medieval mind worked. So we don't just get Richard III and the War of the Roses; we get all of the legends of dragons and werewolves that preoccupied premodern imaginations. We get a world that is prejudiced against Tyrion because the gods must hate him—*why else would the gods have twisted his body?* Even if the gods in Martin's world are mostly veiled (or entirely fraudulent) they are important motivating elements for our favorite characters.[3]

For the same reason, religion is crucially important for the ice-and-fire tapestry. Ancient and medieval religious imaginations become the building blocks for his fantasy. There is no doubt that premodern minds used religion to package rumors, legends, and superstitions.[4] So our favorite rotund writer is rife with religiosity. He is in the business of creating religion because he can't borrow from history without it.

But Martin speaks in a slightly different way about the creation of his religions. He explains that the major religions are "somewhat based on real religions . . . although I don't believe in just doing a one-to-one transformation where I take Islam and file off the serial number and call it 'Mislam' or something. . . . I take certain tenants of the religions but then I take part of this and part of that and I meld them together and I think about it and I add a few imaginative elements."[5]

In his own words, George's method for inventing his religions is more complicated. No simple serial-number filing will do. The process is more imaginative and more cross-pollination is involved. By inventing religions in *A Song of Ice and Fire*, Martin brings complexity to his characters and plotlines.

3. We will return to Tyrion often in this book. So expect more on this topic in the coming chapters.

4. Religion also was prevalent in ideas about farming, eating, marriage, sex, music, society, and all of the other words and things. What we call "religion," they just called "life."

5. George R. R. Martin, "Talks at Google," YouTube video, 1:01:48, conversation with Dan Anthony, July 28, 2011, published August 6, 2011.

So that's what this book is all about. We're convinced that a better grasp on the gods and religions of Martin's world will give us new perspectives on his plots, themes, and settings. Better yet, understanding the mindset of our favorite characters makes them more interesting and reveals more about their underlying motives. We wrote this book because we want to help readers/viewers fall in love with Tyrion, Dany, the Hound, and Arya all over again. Or maybe learn to hate them better and with greater affection. *At least that's what we've been telling people.* The other reason for writing this book is because we needed something to do while we wait impatiently and angrily for *The Winds of Winter*.[6]

6.   George, if you're reading this: *put down the Kindle!* Put it down and go untangle that Meereenese knot. Start by typing these words: "Dany stepped aboard and commanded the captain to set sail." (Just a suggestion.)

HOW TO READ THIS BOOK

This book purports to be a Westerosi travel guide; something between a travel brochure and an airline magazine you'd find in your seatback pocket. Each chapter contains the following structure.

- An epigraph, usually a quote from some philosopher, theologian, or historian
- "Distinctive Elements" and "Key Adherents" that identify the topics covered
- The aforementioned "Travel Guide"
- A "Deep Dive" into a specific religion and/or culture
- A "Historical Backdrop" that compares something in Martin's world to something in real-world history
- "Character Studies," where we examine a particular person from the *A Song of Ice and Fire* books or *Game of Thrones* television series and how they are impacted by the religious culture of the land

- ❧ "Fan Theory Fun," where we present interesting or insane theories that various fans have come up with
- ❧ A "Bird's-Eye View" to examine external influences on Martin's storytelling

These sections are often bolstered by illustrations and text boxes that provide additional or background information. We make use of footnotes to cite sources, develop tangents, and make additional jokes.

A word about citations is warranted. We've followed a citation style that will be familiar to many readers. But we've used a different sort of shorthand for referring to Martin's works. For example, *A World of Ice and Fire* is simply shortened to *World*. When we cite episodes from HBO, we indicate the season and episode numerically and include the title of the episode. For example, S05E08, "Hardhome."

This is a two-volume book. We didn't initially plan it this way; it just sort of evolved into two parts. When we started, we found that we were cutting out too much for the sake of word count and treating too many topics superficially. We also knew that we wanted to keep the price point low. In choosing to write two volumes, we're (1) giving ourselves room to dig as deep as we want and (2) giving our readers the option to try volume 1 and decide whether or not they want to buy the second volume. Volume 1 includes, for example, the old gods, Craster's covenant with the Others, R'hllor, the Seven, and skeptics (among others). Volume 2 includes, for example, Dothraki culture, the Drowned God, the House of Black and White, dragon magic, etc. Volume 2 also includes a glossary of Martin's various snarks and grumkins. We preemptively apologize if you've picked up only a single volume and learned after the fact that it didn't include your favorite fake god/religion. But maybe you should try a different fake god/religion—they say that imaginary variety is the spice of make-believe life.

SPOILERS!

Yea, there be spoilers in them thar chapters. This book is designed for both book readers and show-only watchers alike. In fact, we will often call out references to show-only or book-only events. We decided not to privilege the book canon over the HBO series. But we do detail the differences from time to time. So if you've not yet read the books or you're avoiding the series for the sake of purity, we can't help you. We respect you. But we think you're Patchface-crazy and have milked one poppy too many. Hopefully this book will appeal to both audiences, but we didn't write it spoiler-free.

Finally, this book was written before the airing of HBO's final season and before the publication of *The Winds of Winter* and *Fire and Blood*. That said, enough of Martin's worldbuilding efforts have been published for us to analyze (in some cases, overanalyze) them. While the puzzle hasn't been completed, we've got the corner pieces in place and a good idea of the big picture. This fact also allows us to play with fan theories and do a bit of theory-crafting of our own. So rather than offering the definitive or comprehensive analysis on Martin's gods, we've decided to play in the delightfully gray areas of our incomplete knowledge. This is, after all, a book about religion.

Seeing Green

STARKS, SPIRITS, SQUIRRELS, AND SUPERSIZED SPECIMEN

1

There is in Celtic mythology the notion of "thin places" in the universe where the visible and the invisible world come into their closest proximity. To seek such places is the vocation of the wise and the good— and for those that find them, the clearest communication between the temporal and eternal. Mountains and rivers are particularly favored as thin places marking invariably as they do, the horizontal and perpendicular frontiers. But perhaps the ultimate of these thin places in the human condition are the experiences people are likely to have as they encounter suffering, joy, and mystery.

—PETER J. GOMES

Distinctive Elements
- animism
- thin places
- dirty hippies

Key Adherents
- Ned Stark
- Sansa Stark
- Jojen Reed (now available in convenient, delicious, and mind-expanding paste!)

TRAVEL GUIDE

THE SNOWCAPS AND slopes of the North have attracted adventurous tourists for millennia. Ancient woods, glistening tundra, and the fjords—*oh, the fjords!* But while the gelid beauty of the North is inviting, many Southerners find the culture difficult to navigate. Everything you've heard about these Portlandia savages beyond the Wall is true, and they're committed to keeping the Lands of Always Winter weird. The North is rife with militant musicians, feral feminists, and astral-bodied arborists. You're more likely to find a shaman than a shower. They call themselves the Free Folk and they don't kneel unless it's to scalp a crow. Wildlings are crazy-go-nuts for crow killing. So in packing your holiday wardrobe, avoid taking the black.

If you can get past the anti-authoritarian tribalism, you might find respite among the tree huggers. Chill out among the weirwoods with Leaf the voodoo child and learn the virtues of flower power. Pass the time with sprightly seniors and gentle-giant vegetarians. If hiking is your jam, the trails beyond the Frostfang Mountains are groovy. The vistas of the Fist of the First Men will blow your hair back. For foodies, the regional cuisine is one of a kind. Keep an eye out for the unique street fare in Thenn country. While the vendors can be a bit rough around the edges, all the items on the menu will be locally sourced, free-range, and lack any GMOs, pesticides, or antibiotics. Be deeply skeptical of any claim to be "cruelty free."

Seeing Green: Starks, Spirits, Squirrels, and Supersized Specimen

DEEP DIVE: WUNDERKIND

THE MYTHISTORY OF Westeros begins with gnomish creatures with centuries-long lifespans. Think of Puck from *A Midsummer Night's Dream* then sprinkle a bit of *True Detective* Carcosa worship and you've got the "Children of the Forest." This pint-sized people thrived during the Dawn Age, before the coming of the so-called First Men. The men—having the cultural sensitivity of donkeys—dubbed them "Children."[7] The neighboring giants of the Dawn Age called them "squirrel people." We're not sure which of these labels is more offensive. But determining a self-designation for them is difficult due to the fact that their language remains a mystery. What they called themselves in the early days remains a mystery because their language was notoriously difficult to understand. Early traditions say that they spoke by mimicking the sounds of streams, rolling rocks, and rustling leaves. So communicating even proper names was extremely difficult. We will refer to them as "Children" over the course of this book. But while our fingers type Children, in our hearts we will gurgle, swish, and flutter.

Clearly, Martin wants us to imagine a small, leafy people who look like human children at first glance. Upon first meeting Leaf, Bran Stark wonders if she is a child. But once face-to-face with her, Bran realizes that she is much older (*Dance* 13, Bran II). "Leaf" is the name Bran gives her, as she has leaves for clothing and something like a bird's nest for hair. Alas, it seems that Granola Boy is turning into a damned hippie.

All of the details about the Children's appearance prepare Martin's readers for nature magic and nature worship. This is Martin's way of explaining animism to us without using the term "animism." These leafy people don't just worship trees; they look like squirrels, dress in leaves, and are named "Leaf." Even if he hit us over the head with a pan flute, it couldn't be more obvious that Martin intends to communicate a culture of animism.[8]

It might be more appropriate to call the ritualized life of the Children a worldview or a cosmology rather than a religion. In this understanding of the world, there is almost no distinction between the elements of nature and spirituality. In other words, there is no dividing line

7. Colonizers who perceive aboriginal cultures to be inferior tend to describe these cultures as childlike.

Deep Dive: Wunderkind

8. The term "animism" has fallen out of favor in many anthropological circles. The religious category was developed in the eighteenth and nineteenth centuries by modern Europeans who attempted to classify and label ancient cultures. So ancient people (like the Celts) would not have thought of themselves in these terms. The term, however, was embraced by modern nature spiritualities (like Wicca) in an attempt to part ways with established Western traditions. Martin claims to have patterned the "old gods" after Celtic and Norse systems alongside Wicca. The first two of these are indeed ancient, but Wiccan adaptation of paganism is quite modern. So the rituals and worship of the Children are an amalgam of ancient and modern constructs. As such, the term animism is appropriate. Moreover, Martin himself uses the term "animism" in describing his construct. See Martin, "Talks at Google," YouTube, August 6, 2011.

between sacred and secular (as we might find with the maesters). For cultures like the Children of the Forest, hunting, gathering, eating, worship, and healing are all tied together. Every rock, hill, and stream is animated with divine life (*Game* 66, Bran VII). These gods are numerous and nameless but they are ever-present.

Not every blade of grass, however, is animated equally and some cows are more sacred than others. To illustrate this point with an analogy, let's look East. One of the most ancient cultures of Essos, the Rhoynar, worshipped the great river goddess: Mother Rhoyne. The Rhoynar venerated other gods, too, crab and turtle gods among them. But Mother Rhoyne (a Nile River doppelganger) was among the most powerful forces of nature in the known world. It makes sense, then, that the river goddess would be higher in rank than the other gods in the Rhoynar pantheon. Almost every necessity of life was gathered from the bounty of this river (*World*, "Ten Thousand Ships"). The many people who drew from the Rhoyne naturally thought of her as their big mama. This shows how geography can determine a god's cosmological rank from an animistic perspective.

The Children of the Forest's natural habitat is—and you may find this shocking—the forest. It stands to reason, therefore, that tree gods will be most honored. To drive this point home, Martin's world includes certain elements of nature that defy natural decay. Within the forests of Westeros, weirwood trees live on perpetually if they are left alone (*Dance* 34, Bran III). Like the great River Rhoyne, such trees are seemingly eternal. And if eternal, they require a more robust mythology.

Imagine that you've got an animistic worldview, living among the trees, and one species of tree is seemingly eternal. Chances are good that you'll conclude that the gods of the weirwoods are the most powerful deities of the northern landscape. Greater attention, more earnest prayer, and better sacrifices are owed to such gods. Over time these actions become patterns, and patterns become rituals. Before you know it, you're hanging the entrails of your enemies on their branches. (That's just how slippery slopes work, dude.)[9]

Weirwood groves function like temples for a culture without buildings. The weirwood grove is a sacred place where the veil between the spiritual and physical world is especially permeable. In Celtic terminology, such places are called "thin places." Real-world examples of thin places would include the stone circle at Drombeg or the Hill of Tara tombs. These are both ancient Irish examples. They were most likely considered thin places before the Celts arrived in Ireland. And after the marriage of Celtic and Roman cultures, Celtic Christianity carried on the concept of thin places. The Isle of Iona—the heralded cradle of Christianity in Scotland—is often called a thin place.

Something very similar could be said of Martin's landscape. The Isle of Faces and pinnacle of High Heart (more on these below) are examples of thin places. In such places, the Children carve faces on the weirwood trees in order to commune with the divine. While all of nature is infused with spirituality, certain locations have thinner time-space fabrics and are therefore closer to the gods.

9.   It may be helpful here to point out the difference between animism and naturalistic pantheism. Pantheism holds that the universe and God are identical. Or, formulated slightly differently, it holds that the same divine life force pervades all of nature to form a summative unity (compare, e.g., Taoism). The Children of the Forest fit better within an animistic system, as they believe that particular spirits inhabit particular elements of nature. For a pantheist, there would be no need to single out a river goddess or a tree god as special. These two cosmologies do sometimes overlap, varying from culture to culture.

Drombeg Stone Circle

In carving faces into weirwood bark, the Children created a permanent connection with the gods. (How the old gods initially came into being is a topic for *Gods of Thrones*, volume 2. For now we will just point out that greenseers enjoy a "second life" after they die by merging with the trees they inhabit; *Dance* 34, Bran III.) The sap of weirwood is crimson, giving the appearance of eyes and mouths that drip blood. *Who doesn't want to cozy up to a dryad weeping bloody tears?* Once the white bark was punctured, these "Heart Tree" faces became conduits between thin places. Such faces don't simply represent a personalized portrait of a nameless god. The Children carved eyes into these trees so that the gods could witness their devotion (*World*, "The Dawn Age").[10]

The Children employed "greenseers" (very much like shamans) to mediate their thin places. Greenseers are able to see beyond the strictures of time and space. On occasion, they wield the power of the spiritual world in ways that seem magical to outsiders. This brings us to the light topic of blood sacrifice. But before addressing the hilarity of human smoothies and circling entrails, let's turn our attention to the vegetarian giants of the North.

It will have to remain a mystery why the shy giants of the North warred with the wise Children of the Forest. This part of Dawn Age history is murky. The most likely answer relates to the territorial nature of the Children. We know that they will go to war to defend their sacred trees. Couple this with the fact that the giants are known for roaming and taking whatever they want, and you've got a problem (*World*, "The Dawn Age"). Whatever the reason, the giants and the Children were often at loggerheads.

During periods of war, the hunters of the Children—called Forest Dancers—become warriors. The fact that their bows are made from weirwood (*Game* 66,

10. If thought of in Norse mythological terms, the cosmos is made up of nine worlds and they are networked within the branches and roots of the World Tree. Because these worlds are connected, there are certain gateway places between worlds. Think of the Bifröst, the famous rainbow bridge that allows the Mighty Thor to venture from Asgard to Midgard, better known to us mortals as "Earth."

Bran VII) is telling, as it reminds us that all life patterns are connected to the spirit world. Again, there is no distinction between sacred and secular in the culture of the Children. Weirwood can be used to enhance life and defend life. Greenseers therefore had a double function: they were shamans who communed with spirits and they were spies who used the conduits between thin places to gather wartime intelligence.

Deep Dive: Wunderkind

You might think that being able to peer into the future through the eyes of the Heart Trees would be a dominating wartime advantage. But we guess that greenseers were quite limited in their ability to predict the future. Otherwise, the Children would not have been driven to retreat by the giants and, eventually, the First Men. An obvious analogue here is Melisandre, to whom visions of possible futures appear, but who sometimes fails in her interpretation. Or it could be that Martin's world-building efforts are intentionally vague for a reason: *characters who know the future completely are no fun*. Whatever the greenseers predictive abilities are, it seems that the Heart Trees are more valuable as spying mechanisms. This is why the First Men eventually felled all Heart Trees in the South. Seemingly—once the Heart Trees are destroyed—the Children's wartime prowess diminishes significantly.

By far the greatest act of weaponized weirwood wonderment is found in the legend of the "Hammer of the Waters." This legend is an etiology (a story that explains the cause of something) accounting for the sunken land bridge between Westeros and Essos. When the First Men colonized Westeros, they threatened the forests. This resulted in two thousand years of war between the colonizers and the aboriginals. To impede colonization, the Children endeavored to crush the path the First Men took from Essos to Dorne. Their greenseers performed ritual

blood offerings by the hundreds (perhaps sacrificing their own offspring) to summon "the Hammer." The details of this legend are vague, but the Hammer seems to have taken the form of a great flood (the Rhoynar have a similar legend about weaponizing the Rhoyne River). This act rendered what was once called the Arm of Dorne to a channel of islands. A similar act of blood magic was employed to create the swamplands in the middle of Westeros (*World*, "The Coming of the First Men").

Deep Dive: Wunderkind

These legends of blood rituals and divine intervention lead us to conclude that the battles for Westeros were first and foremost holy wars. But to avoid anachronism, keep in mind that (to the ancient way of thinking) *holy war* was just called *war*. It is common today to view war as a terrible but sometimes necessary evil. Most Western minds consider warfare motivated by religion to be repugnant (the authors of this book included). But for ancient peoples—and the Children are cast as such—warfare without divine support was considered futile.[11] In times of great need, blood ritual was sometimes used to get the attention of the gods and to curry their favor.

11. See William T. Cavanaugh, *The Myth of Religious Violence* (Oxford: Oxford University Press, 2009).

Soon after the Children hammered the waters, a truce was made between the aboriginals and the colonizers. This is often referred to simply as "the Pact." The First Men were allowed to colonize most of Westeros as long as they left the forested areas to the Children. Most importantly, the men vowed to refrain from cutting down any more sacred trees. And just as the war between groups was "holy," the pact that ended the war required a religious ceremony involving—*you guessed it*—deciduous horticulture.

In the center of a large lake called the "Gods Eye" was an island with several weirwoods. Such an island is a classic example of a thin place. The Children of the Forest and the First Men met here to create their peace covenant. The greenseers carved faces on every weirwood on the island, thereby ensuring that the Pact was witnessed by the gods several times over. Thereafter the island was named the "Isle of Faces" and a monastic order was created to tend, protect, and commune with these Heart Trees. This order was named the "Green Men." Due to the order's isolation, little is known about them save rumors. Some imagine them to be green-skinned magicians with leaves for hair and antlers. If so, they probably don't find christianmingle. com very useful.[12]

12. For Green Men lookalikes we recommend farmersonly.com. "City folks just don't get it."

Gundestrup Cauldron: This silver cauldron (ca. 200 BCE–300 CE) features the image of an antlered man, perhaps the Celtic deity "Cernunnos." Courtesy of Wikimedia Commons.

What followed was a four thousand-year era of relative peace between the warring factions. Moreover, the First Men adopted the gods of the Children. Because of Martin's interest in the Celts, the three iterations of sacred "thin places" in Ireland is an apt analog:[13]

13. By appealing to this analog, we don't intend to negate other analogs. As we discuss elsewhere, Martin builds his world by creating amalgams of historical analogies.

1. The pre-Celtic Irish folk consecrate thin places;

2. These thin places are adopted by the Celts;

3. The same thin places are appropriated by Celtic Christianity (although the new religion supersedes animism).

Consider now the parallel stages of Martin's northern animism:

A. The Children consecrate Heart Trees;

B. The First Men adopt Heart Trees as places of prayer;

C. After the arrival of the Andals, the folk of the North continue to revere the "old gods" (although the new religion supersedes animism).

The fact that Martin associates the Andals' religion—the Faith of the Seven—with Christianity is also telling. Once "the Seven" are established as the state religion, those who continue to practice the ways of the First Men are now practitioners of the "old ways" (as Ned Stark famously tells his son Bran; S01E01, "Winter Is Coming").

Finally, what the maesters call the Age of Heroes concludes with religious syncretism (the marriage of multiple sacred traditions into a new religious ethos). This syncretism in Martin's world is heard loud and clear in the phrase "the old Gods and the new." These two systems may well be uncomfortably aligned but they are intermingled nonetheless. Notice, for example, that the High Septon's staff is made of weirwood (*Feast* 7, Cersei II). In this case, the high seat of the new religion appropriates something sacred from the old gods. Conversely, the Starks preserve both a weirwood grove and a sept (dedicated to the Seven) within the walls of Winterfell. Indeed, the marriage of Ned Stark and Catelyn Tully is an illustration of how these worlds collided. Although Catelyn is literally married into the "old ways," she worships at her own sept and feels like an outsider in the weirwood grove. And despite their level of spiritual comfort or discomfort, Ned and Catelyn sire a greenseer of uncanny ability.

HISTORICAL BACKDROP: TREE SPRITS IN MYTH AND RELIGION

THE IDEA OF tree spirits is at least as old as the ancient Greeks. In Greek mythology "naiads" (meaning "ladies of the trees") functioned as nature spirits and were also associated with bodies of water. Dryad literally means "oak nymph."

Hinduism, Buddhism, and Jainism venerate tree-related spirits called *yakshis*. When involved in the life of humans, these spirits are generally benevolent or neutral. The *diwata* of Philippine mythology can refer to generic spirits but has come to be associated more specifically with tree spirits. Most mythologies think of these spirits as feminine. In the Middle East, the Druze (a minority religious group in Israel) associate certain holy trees with lives of their prophets and religious leaders.

Tolkien's variation on tree spirits is that they can be awake or, more often, asleep. Trees can be benevolent but they can also be malicious and dangerous. Tolkien also employs tree shepherds called the Ents, which are anthropomorphic (human-looking) trees. These trees with human faces may be a partial inspiration for Martin's character Brynden "Bloodraven" Rivers, who has merged his body with a sacred tree to enhance his prophetic abilities.

CHARACTER STUDY: NED

THERE HE IS: the famous Eddard "Ned" Stark, praying in the godswood of Winterfell. This grove is where the First Men worshipped before the Southern religions were brought to Westeros. The Heart

Tree in the grove's center has the carving of a face on the trunk. The image has been there for millennia and will be there as long as a Stark remains in Winterfell.

The Chief Druid: This 18th-century etching depicts a druid holding an oak branch. Courtesy of Wikimedia Commons.

Honest, grim Ned. Honorable, pious Ned. Stupid, pathetic, soon-to-be-headless Ned. He is among the most beloved and belittled characters in George R. R. Martin's world. Many fans of *A Game of Thrones* are convinced that Ned's political ineptitude is a genetic disorder among Stark men. They have a talent for swordplay, brooding, and battle tactics, but when it comes to intrigue they are glacially slow. Martin rarely places witty banter on the lips of these dullards. The slogan "Winter is coming" nearly exhausts the Stark vocabulary. So it is not surprising that the Starks do not articulate their religion in great detail. It is, however, ingrained in them. For all of their failings, they are devoted to the old gods.

Ned's religion is something close to animism—specifically, Celtic Druidry. In this view of the world, trees, rivers, and animals are animated by the spirit world. Tree worship, which is central to Stark religion, is a dead give-away. Their devotion to the weirwood is more than mere ritual. In praying, they expect the ancient spirits within to hear them and see them. The Starks have literally built their lives around the sacred grove. The architecture of Winterfell was designed around the godswood.

Many cultures that contain elements of animism also venerate ancestral spirits. While the Starks do not worship their ancestors per se, they do pay them homage in the Winterfell crypts. Ancient Stark kings and more recent lords of Winterfell there sit carved in stone, with iron swords drawn across their laps, eternally vigilant against restless spirits.

Animistic peoples tend to be highly tribal. Not only is Ned's family tribal, they consider themselves as tight as a pack of wolves. Their house sigil is the legendary direwolf. (In Latin, *canis dirus* means "dreadful dog.") In Martin's world, the beast is more than a totem. Some Starks are spiritually connected to these animals, even able to occupy their bodies while in dream states. During seasons of winter and war the Starks become even more protective of "the pack."

Because Ned Stark is most associated with the title *A Game of Thrones* (the first book of the series), he is generally judged by his inability to play politics. Ned fails to recognize that he's even playing the game until it's too late. It's almost as if he thinks he's in a detective novel. By this measure, Ned is the ultimate loser. Winning the game involves keeping the right secrets and spinning the most advantageous deceptions. Ned, by contrast, is determined to learn the truth, tell the truth, and be true to his honor. While his rigid refusal to play the game invites the ire and lament of fans, Martin foreshadows Ned's rigidity early in the story. No doubt, this makes Ned's final act all the more surprising and vexing.

Because Martin has adapted Celtic animism, we should remember that the Druids have a historic relationship to tree spirits. Druidic groups are often referred to as "groves." This self-identification reminds us that Druids once worshipped among the trees (adherents of neo-Druidism still do). It is also telling that the word *Druid* literally means "oak seer." It comes from the Old Celtic word *derwos*. But this word has a double meaning: the first is *oak tree*; the second is *truth*. So a Druid is one who "knows the oak" and "knows the truth." Likewise, the Anglo-Saxon word *treow* also means both "tree" and "truth."

A story from Scottish lore shows the connection between trees and truth in the medieval mind. This story is often referred to as "Thomas the Rhymer" and is based on a thirteenth-century poet named Thomas de Ercildoun. Thomas meets the "Queen of fair Elfland" under a fairy tree. Such trees were thought of as spiritual gateways. The Queen leads Thomas into Elfland, where he receives a tongue that cannot lie. He also gets a new coat and some snazzy green shoes (i.e., fancy lad school). The historical Thomas was known for his career as a prophet. With this in mind, this fairytale is an origin story about how he got his super-truth-telling power.

From a modern perspective, it is easy to construe this superpower as a liability. *Who wouldn't get in trouble with a tongue that couldn't lie?* We have no idea if Martin is aware of the Thomas the Rhymer story. But we guess that if this story was reframed for modern audiences, Thomas would probably end up like Ned Stark.

More importantly, there was a strong association between trees and truth in the medieval mind. Given Martin's religious worldbuilding, Ned's commitment to truth may be foreshadowed by his tree worship. Martin has used the religious setting of the North to fortify Ned's character. He is, *as a person rooted in truth*, simply ill equipped to play the game of thrones.

DEEP DIVE: ARE GIANTS JUST BIG ANIMALS?

According to the historians of the Citadel and the records of the Night's Watch, the giants of the Dawn Age were simpletons. These great bipeds— covered in fur and twelve feet tall—seem more zoological than anthropological. Three criteria go into this assessment: (1) the giants did not work with metal nor did they show any knowledge of it; (2) they used only caves or tall trees for shelter; (3) they seemed to lack kings and lords (*World*, "The Dawn Age"). This third point is reiterated from a Free Folk perspective by Tormund: giants, like the mammoths they ride, do not have kings, nor do they kneel to their leaders. Tormund compares giants to mammoths, snow bears, or whales, none of which play with crowns and thrones (*Storm* 15, Jon II).

It's possible that giants lack a clear social hierarchy. But it's also possible that the men in Martin's world just can't discern any ruling class among the giants. So we ought to ask: Does the lack of a ruler warrant the zoological comparison? Put another way: Do these giants lack culture?

The showrunners of *Game of Thrones* seem to indicate otherwise. Mag the Mighty is a case in point. After Mag is killed at the Battle of Castle Black, he is remembered as a king. Mance Rayder claims that Mag is the end of a bloodline that extends back to the Dawn Age (S04E10, "The Children"). This show-only detail portrays giant culture in terms of hereditary titles and leadership. Here we might have an instance where the showrunners part ways with book canon. According to *A Storm of Swords,* the other giants follow Mag, but there is no clear concept of kingship among them. Mag is called "king" in the same way that George Costanza refers to his big toe as the "captain of the toes."

While it's near impossible to answer the question of kingship with any certainty, we think we can put to rest the question of culture. There are, in fact, two clear indications of giant culture in book canon.

First, the giants of the Dawn Age are known for their burial sites (*World,* "The Dawn Age"). This fact suggests *ritual,* which is a strong indicator of culture. It is also worth noting that burial ritual usually fits hand-in-glove with a belief in the afterlife. But we need to tread lightly here because we have no other indication of a giant mythology or religion.

Second, Mag makes a joke at Jon Snow's expense. Mag suggests that Jon is a maiden girl and then laughs (*Storm* 15, Jon 11). If language is not a clear enough indication, joke telling requires an advanced use of language. So humor—joking especially—is a decisive indication of culture. There can be no doubt that the giants of Martin's world are more than mere beasts.

Deep Dive: Are Giants Just Big Animals?

WE'VE BEEN TEASING the theory known as "Jojen Paste" throughout this chapter. This theory reminds us that the Children of the Forest aren't the cute and cuddly Hobbits they appear to be. And the Three-Eyed Crow is no Treebeard. For a variety of reasons, it's also one of the more controversial theories among the fan base.

In *Dance*, Bran is fed a special paste made of weirwood seed and sap by the Children. The Three-Eyed Crow explains that the paste will bind Bran to the trees and supercharge his greenseeing gifts. It is served to him in a weirwood bowl decorated with tiny carved faces. The paste is white, and streaked through with what Bran thinks is sap. From Bran's perspective, it looks like red veins running through the thickened paste. By torchlight it has the appearance of fresh blood.

Bran finds the taste disagreeable at first but as he continues to eat develops an appetite and greedily devours it. The paste tastes better with every bite.[14] Afterward the Bloodraven bids him to slip his mind into the trees around him as he has done many times before with his direwolf and Hodor. When he does so, he is treated to intense visions of his family, the past, reaching back into prehistory.

After this experience, Jojen is not seen or heard from again. The implication is that the Children murdered the fellow greenseer Jojen, and mixed his blood into the paste so that by blood magic—or perhaps even by consuming Jojen's power himself—Bran would get stronger. It's certainly a creepy idea, and casts the mentor of our little hero in a very unflattering, ghoulish light. But is it true?

14. Compare Daenerys' reaction to drinking shade of the evening as the Warlocks' guest in the House of the Undying (*Clash* 63, Daenerys v).

If you're a show watcher, the answer is *of course not.* We saw Jojen die back in season 4 (S04E10, "The Children"), and while *Thrones* does not lack for ambiguous cliffhanger "deaths," this was decidedly not one of them. The poor boy was literally mercy-exploded by the Children's fireball magic after he was brutally gutted by a pack of knife-wielding wights. In the show, Jojen Paste is definitely not a thing. Case closed.

But if you see the book as a higher order of canon, or at the very least, an alternate narrative, Jojen Paste bears a closer look. Because things *just ain't right* with Jojen in *Dance.* In fact, the entire Bran III chapter is full of foreboding, sacrificial imagery. Martin uses the moon's state to relate the passage of time during the chapter, but note how it is described. First, "a crescent, thin and sharp as the blade of a knife,"[15] then "a black hole in the sky," before finally "fat and full." One possible reading is a three-part symbolism: a butcher carving up a roast, ravenously hungry, which is then fully consumed.

15. Unless stated otherwise, all quotes in this section come from *Dance* 34, Bran III.

Jojen at this point has achieved a huge part of his mission, delivering Bran to the Three-Eyed Crow; "My task was to get you here. My part in this is done." But far from being happy or accomplished, he is described as sad, haunted, and weary. Certainly the long trek north was harrowing and took a toll on him, but he isn't killed by wights. Rather, Jojen is cared for by the Children; "Food and fire and rest had helped restore him after the ordeals of their journey."

Jojen has said since *Clash* that he has foreseen the day of his death, frequently assuring his sister Meera during their perils that "this is not the day I die." Now, however, he seems fixated on his own death. Jojen explains to Bran in Bloodraven's cave that the old "singers of the forest" eventually die and become part of the weirwoods themselves, a prospect that frightens Bran. Meera interrupts him, "Jojen, you're scaring him," to which he replies, "He is not the one who needs to be afraid."

Jojen becomes withdrawn, retreating to the mouth of the cave daily to stare out endlessly, shivering. When Bran asks about his strange behavior, Meera explains that her brother wants desperately to go home, but that "he will not even try and fight his fate." Jojen is convinced that his greendreams have predicted his final outcome. What fate does his sister want him to fight, and why does it seem connected to leaving the cave and going home? *Could it be that Meera doesn't want her brother to become a protein shake?*

Jojen and Meera are not seen again in *Dance*. Bran looks for them, eager to share with them the things that he's seen in his visions, "but their snug alcove in the rock was cold and empty." Instead, Bran sees a final vision in the chapter. He sees a man being sacrificed before Winterfell's weirwood tree in ancient times: "As his life flowed out of him in a red tide, Brandon Stark could taste the blood."

Having already acknowledged the show's role in debunking this theory, we must also point out that the Children are seen performing a human sacrifice in the show, too. Using blood magic to achieve their ends is consistent with their character. The show runs ahead of the books by showing how the Children created the White Walkers in the first place by stabbing a very unwilling man in the chest with an obsidian dagger (S06E05, "The Door").

For now it's up to the individual reader or viewer to decide how they feel about the evidence and its harrowing implications. The matter will probably not be settled one way or another until *The Winds of Winter* finally blow into bookstores.

BIRD'S-EYE VIEW:
THE INK IS DRY [16]

IN OUR DEEP dive into Celtic "thin places," we infected your Borg-collective mind with the suggestion that sacred trees are time-space conduits. By tapping into tree-spirit technology, Bran is able to astrally project his ass to different places and different times. Once Martin had established this Celtic tech, it was only a matter of time before he sprinkled some sci-fi magic into his fantasy cauldron. Season 6 of *Game of Thrones* brought this hoary plot device to fruition and—as time paradoxes tend to do—has created chaos in the fan hivemind.

From T. H. White's Merlin, who lives backwards through time and remembers the future, to the Terminator hunting down Sarah Connor, storytellers have wrestled with balancing the inherently interesting and powerful mechanic of time manipulation, with its ability to cause unsolvable paradoxes and rip open plot holes that no amount of souped-up DeLoreans can mend.

Bran, under the tutelage of Brynden "Bloodraven" Rivers, the Three-Eyed Crow, sees visions of the past, including his father's exploits at the Tower of Joy. There, Ned found his sister dying after having given birth to one Aegon Targaryen, a.k.a. Jon Snow. As Bran watches his father and stalwart companions win their duel with the three members of the Kingsguard stationed there to protect Rhaegar and Lyanna's secret, he calls out, "Father!" Lord Stark pauses and turns back, as if he almost—but not quite—hears Bran.

Bran is astonished that his father can hear him, and wants to return to the past to try to establish communication. The Three-Eyed Crow instructs him that "the past is already written, the ink is dry" (S06E04, "Book of the

16. In this book, we will conclude each chapter with a "Bird's-Eye View" where we take a critical look at Martin's story and compare it with other kinds of stories, theories, and statements of authorial intention. Sometimes our Bird's-Eye Views are intentionally provocative and political. We realize that these topics aren't going please everyone and may, at times, attract ire. If you need to skip ahead to the next chapter, no hard feelings. Words are Wind.

Stranger"). In other words, Bran can go back, observe, and learn from the past, but he can't influence it. This is already a powerful ability, allowing Bran to uncover past lies and deceptions, or witness events unfolding that provide valuable insight and context to the present.

☙ *Excursus: Words Are Wind* ☙

Martin's use of characters hearing the wind might help us identify evidence of potential time travel: (1) After Bran cries "father" at the Tower of Joy, Bloodraven is dismissive. "Maybe, maybe he heard the wind." (2) On the day that the Starks find a litter of direwolf pups, Jon claims to hear something; whereas Bran can only hear the gentle rustling of wind (*Game* 1, Bran 1). (3) During her service at Harrenhal, Arya asks the old gods to tell her what to do. As she prays before the godswood, she thinks she hears a voice like her father reminding her that "the lone wolf dies, but the pack survives" (*Clash* 64, Arya X). (4) While Theon serves Ramsay as Reek, he thinks he hears voices in the wind speaking to him in proximity to the Heart Tree in the godswood of Winterfell. This happens twice. The first time, he describes the voice as "faint as rustling leaves, as cold as hate" (*Dance* 37, "The Prince of Winterfell"). The second time he hears them, they seemingly inspire him to try to gird his fractured identity as Theon and later attempt to save himself and Jeyne Poole by jumping from the battlements of Winterfell (*Dance* 46, "A Ghost in Winterfell").[17]

---

17. Since we're this far down the wormhole, try some of this Wesley Crusher-flavored paste we've concocted: when Mirr Maz Duur is communing with the spirit world, Dany sees figures dancing around. One appears to be a man wreathed in flame and one is the "shadow of a great wolf" (*Game* 64, Daenerys VIII). Clearly a "great wolf" is a Stark symbol in Martin's world. Could it be that some greenseeing Stark is present during the birth of Dany's child and the stupefaction of Drogo? And wouldn't we find ourselves in an interesting time loop if Dany's dragonish, deformed baby was transported away and raised by some other family? (More on this in a future chapter.)

But later, when Bran is using his powers to observe the day his father left Winterfell as a boy to become a ward in the Vale, the Night King mounts an all-out assault on the Bloodraven's Entish hideout. This is when things get a bit hasty. While still locked in the vision, Bran hears Meera's screams to warg into Hodor, and obeys.[18] The confluence of Bran using his powers both within the visions of the past and in the present causes something strange to happen.

Bran orders Hodor to "hold the door!" Using his deep-dish, two-slice bulk to anchor the door, Hodor is able to keep the horde of undead blocked behind the rear exit of the cave. But while Hodor is jamming the door, Bran accidently butt dials himself into to the younger Hodor. In other words, Bran wargs into Hodor in the past. Young Hodor, who we learn has an actual name, Wylis, is a young stable boy. More importantly, young Wylis doesn't seem to suffer any of the cognitive impairments that characterize present-day Hodor. The power of Bran's warging ability causes Wylis to have a violent seizure, as he repeatedly murmurs "hold the door," slurring it until he is reduced to whimpering "ho'door, ho'door, ho'door" (S06E05, "The Door"). The psychic strain on Wylis' mind is enough to reduce him to the simple but well-hung dude that we've grown to know and love.[19]

Tragically, Bran struggles with the realization that not only has he forced Hodor to sacrifice himself to save Bran and Meera but that in doing so he robbed Hodor of a normal life. This is also the episode that proved to some fans that the Bloodraven is a liar: Bran can absolutely influence the past.

But did he? In science fiction, there are several flavors of time travel, and what most separates them (beyond the fantastic technology or magic that mechanically enables

18. In retrospect, Bran really missed a wide-open "one does not simply warg into Hodor" opportunity. Sure, he's young, and obviously under duress, but c'mon. It was right there.

19. There is some fan-fueled speculation that the fate of Wylis/Hodor mirrors that of the "mad king" Aerys. In his later years, Aerys is known for losing his mind and shouting, "Burn them all!" (S01E03, "Lord Snow"). Yet he wasn't born mad; in his younger days he is described as intelligent, charming, generous, handsome, and resolute. What if Bran tried to visit Aerys and talk sense to him, or subtly nudge him away from the path that led to the deaths of his grandfather and uncle? Or perhaps what drove Aerys mad was the Bloodraven's own clumsy attempts to influence the king, which led to disaster. Or maybe he was merely trying to warn Aerys of the threat of the White Walkers and how to defeat them, which is why the mad king is reduced to screaming "burn them all" in much the same way Wylis is only capable of saying "hodor." If so, the experience led to the destruction of Bloodraven's own house, and taught him the futility of such an endeavor. This is the lesson he tried to impart to Bran.

it) is how malleable the past is to change the present or future. The more rigid a universe's concept of time is, the harder it becomes to change the past.

Seeing Green:
Starks, Spirits, Squirrels,
and Supersized Specimen

For example, in the classic Ray Bradbury short story "The Sound of Thunder," a wealthy man travels back in time on safari to hunt the mighty *Tyrannosaurus rex*. The man has paid a considerable sum of money for time scouts to go back and tag an animal that will die of natural causes (land slide, falling tree, struck by lightning, etc.) later that day, minimizing damage to the time stream. The hunters must also hunt on an elevated, levitating platform to keep them from contaminating the past. As one might expect, things do not go as planned. In the chaos of the hunt, the hunter accidentally steps off the platform and tumbles into the forest below. The dinosaur eventually is killed, moments before the tree that would have killed it lands on its Jurassic noggin. All seems fine, but on returning to his timeline, the hunter discovers the future has changed. When he examines his boots, the hunter finds a crushed ancient butterfly smeared on his sole. The butterfly's untimely death was apparently enough to cause massive changes to his world eons later. Thus Bradbury's notion of a malleable past and possible futures is flexible to a fault.

Contrast Bradbury's notion of time with what is probably the oldest time-travel story ever told. In the Talmud—a post-biblical Jewish text—God and Moses are having a chat. They're discussing the future of Israel's education. God tells Moses about a future rabbi named Akiba ben Joseph, who will be a genius. Akiba will be able to interpret Jewish legal texts in ways that Moses can't even imagine yet. This intrigues Moses, and he asks to travel into the future to see this guy. God obliges. He only has to "walk backwards" and he finds himself in the back of Akiba's classroom. Moses recognizes that his own level of understanding pales in comparison. Poor Moses can't even keep up with Akiba's students. Then he suggests that God might change his mind and give the Torah to Akiba instead. In other words, Moses' inferiority complex makes him want to change the past so that he never receives the Ten Commandments. God refuses and tells Moses to shut his big, fat mouth, "Silence! I've already decided!" Then God—and this is just mean—reveals Akiba's fate. Mr. Super Genius ends up getting butchered.[20] Moses throws God some shade and says, "Is this what people get for studying Torah?!" God replies again, "I've already decided!"[21] Seemingly, the author of this story thinks that God's plan is rigid. Moses' time travel can't change the past or the future. He can only ever be a passive observer of an unchanging timeline. *The ink is dry.*

20. While not detailed in this story, Akiba was flayed to death by Romans in the early second century CE.

21. Babylonian Talmud, tractate Menahoth 29b.

Now consider a modern classic: the *Futurama* episode "Roswell That Ends Well." In this adventure, Fry travels back in time and happens to meet his many times great-grandfather Enos Fry, and winds up accidentally killing him. Everyone expects Fry to vanish à la Dave and Linda McFly. But Fry remains unfaded and ready to party like Marty. Later it is revealed that Fry, after a few stiff drinks, seduces his own grandmother, effectively becoming his own grandfather. The professor concludes the only possible way this could have happened is if Fry had *always* traveled back in time and become his own ancestor.

The core idea here is that if you manage to travel back in time you cannot change the past, because if you did, you could threaten your own existence and not be able to go back in time to threaten it in the first place.

We guess that Martin's notion of time is on the rigid side. Most often, Bran is just a passive observer (like Moses). And when Bran is more actively involved, he is forced to do what the rigid past demands of him (like Fry). Bran did not create a new timeline. Hodor always suffered brain damage, because Bran always travels back in time to cause it. There is no "ideal" timeline where Wylis grows up, marries the cute milkmaid that he'd always exchanged shy glances with across the Winterfell courtyard, and becomes the Stark kennelmaster. Never happened; *never could have happened.* That's not the only way time travel *has* to work, but it appears to be the way things work in Martin's universe. In short, there will be no Bradburyesque butterfly stomping in Martin's world.

At the time of this writing, we're still lacking two books and one half-season of television. But as it stands, we must conclude that in Martin's world, the ability to go back, perceive, and interact with the past has important limitations. Time travelers cannot *change* the past. However, even being a mute observer of the past is still an extremely powerful ability. This sort of greenseeing is useful for catching Littlefinger in a deadly deception, keeping tabs on what the Night King is up to, and finding out Jon Snow's true identity. But going back in time and preventing the Children from creating the Night King in the first place will most likely forever be out of Bran's reach. We're reminded of Stephen Hawking, who famously threw a lavish party for any potential time travelers with the catch that he only sent out invitations after the party happened. Nobody came.[22]

To those still convinced the *Song* will end with some form of *Doctor Whovian,* wibbly-wobbly, timey-wimey stuff happening, we have to ask: If Bran *could* eventually unmake the Night King, then why *hasn't* he?

22. PSA: Future time travelers wanting to make amends for snubbing the author of *A Brief History of Time* at the possible cost of creating an unresolvable time paradox can attend the party on June 28, 2009, at the Earth coordinates 52° 12' 21" N, 0° 7' 4.7" E.

Great Thralls of Fire
THE RELIGION OF R'HLLOR

2

I offer my sacrifice and homage to thee, Oh Fire, as a good offering, and an offering with our hail of salvation, as an offering of praise with benedictions, to thee, Oh Fire, Oh Wise Lord's son!

—ZARATHUSTRA

Distinctive Elements
- belief in two warring gods
- hope for the end of the world
- evangelistic
- obnoxious

Key Adherents
- Beric Dondarrion
- Melisandre of Asshai
- Stannis Baratheon
- Thoros of Myr

TRAVEL GUIDE

IF YOU FIND yourself in the company of a Lord of Light lackey on the kingsroad, do your best to avoid the following two topics: the old gods and the new and the Prince That Was Promised. Either topic may land you in some sexy-but-creepy dogmatic dialogue. If these topics cannot be avoided, it is best to avoid R'hllor worshippers altogether.

In Volantis, however, the religion is nearly impossible to avoid, as the city is home to the most impressive of the Red Temples. Take care if approaching the temple for a tour. It is guarded by an army of slaves (exactly 1,000 of them) called the Fiery Hand. Each slave's face is tattooed with flames. There can be no doubt that the tattoo parlors in Volantis are among the best in Essos. If the temple's guardians are impressive, the structure itself is even more so. The Red Temple is a massive complex of imposing towers, high domes, and endless stairs, all in fiery colors of red, yellow, and orange. It's three times the size of the Great Sept of Baelor in King's Landing, but who's keeping score? (*World,* "Volantis").

DEEP DIVE:
FULL OF TERRORS

IN WESTEROS, CIRCA the Baratheon period, it is common parlance to refer to "the old gods and the new." This idiom points to two different belief systems: the nature gods of the North and the relatively newer Faith of the Seven. But these words are heresy to the ears of Melisandre, the Red Priestess. She will be quick to point out that *there is only one, true God:* R'hllor, the Lord of Light. And she follows this dogma with slavish dedication. Using the language of game theory, we could call this a "zero-sum game" religion. If there is only one true religion, all other religions are valueless fables.

But Melisandre's math is off by 50 percent, even if judged by her own theology. R'hllor has a Dark Side counterpart, the so-called "Great Other." In her world of binary opposites, the difference between the two deities is the difference between warmth and cold, light and dark, waking and sleeping, life and death. This is not quite a yin and yang scenario, because Melisandre isn't looking for balance; she's hoping for a total eclipse of the Great Other. R'hllor worship is more like Jedi religion. Jedi masters may talk about "balance" but Jedi masters are liars.

It would be more accurate to say that the religion of R'hllor is a dichotomous theistic faith: the belief in two great deities at war. Like many ancient theologies, the adherents of this faith believe that the great divine war is mirrored by earthly battles. As such, the happenings of heaven impact earthly realities and vice versa. In the case of Melisandre's theology, the Great Other must be nearly as powerful as her own god or the divine war wouldn't be much of a fight.

Even so, the name of the Great Other is never spoken and Melisandre rarely speaks about this deity. She does refer to the Others (a.k.a. White Walkers) as the "cold children" of the Great Other (*Storm* 78, Samwell v). But we know little else about the Lord of Light's evil twin. We hope and pray that if the Great Other ever shows up on screen he will be played by David Hasselhoff with a Zappa mustache.

The followers of R'hllor tend to be cocksure in their faith. They believe that their Lord is the grandmaster of the chessboard that is the game of thrones. They are so certain of their faith that they're on a global mission for converts. As a result of this mission, R'hllor worshippers are from all over the map. For example: Melisandre from Asshai; Beric Dondarrion from Blackhaven; Lady Selyse from Brightwater Keep; Thoros from Myr. Thoros, for example, initially relocated to Westeros on a mission to convert Robert Baratheon (Bobby B. wasn't all that interested).

This is the sort of religion that features street preachers. The high priest, Benerro, is seen preaching to anyone who will listen on the streets of Volantis. He preaches that

Daenerys Targaryen is the reincarnation of a great hero of religious tradition. Benerro exhorts all who will listen to support her cause (*Dance* 33, Tyrion VII).

This leads us to the so-called Prince That Was Promised. Before getting to the framework of the prophecy, the scribes from Asshai who preserved this bit of dogma need grammatical help. While *"that* was promised" is fine, it would be better rendered *"who* was promised." Also, there is some dispute among grammarians as to the gender of the "prince." Some argue that the prophecy is gender neutral (S07E02, "Stormborn"). If so, it would be better rendered "the *one* who was promised." But don't try to correct Melisandre on either point. She is focused with red-hot passion that a warrior-king figure will emerge to save the day. The Red Priestess is willing to do anything for her hunk-a-hunk of burning love, murdering fools and grammar alike.

So certain is Melisandre of this prince (also called the Lord's Chosen or the Warrior of Light) that her faith is contagious. Adopting her faith can mean severed family ties and blood-soaked battlefields. An occasional human sacrifice doesn't bother her if she believes it will gain the favor of her Lord. Melisandre demonstrates undeniable power, including a command of magic (see below). But her greatest power is political. If she can convince a royal claimant that he or she is the promised champion, the convinced military leader will play the game of thrones all the more aggressively. Many of the key battles of the Baratheon period simply would not have unfolded how they did without Melisandre's provocation. When we first meet her in the story, she is convinced that Stannis Baratheon is the prince she's been waiting for.

According to the prophetic lore of Asshai, the storied Prince That Was Promised will be born of "salt and smoke."

This prophecy is just ambiguous enough to be applied to a wide array of possible candidates. Perhaps providing more clarity (but not much), this champion will wield a flaming sword called "Lightbringer." This Warrior of Light is a bit like an expected Jedi, bringing balance to the Force, wielding a lightsaber. But in Martin's world we're looking at the hope for royal reincarnation. R'hllor's chosen warrior will embody the return of a character named Azor Ahai.

Deep Dive: Full of Terrors

To make one of Old Nan's very long stories short, Azor Ahai first lived millennia ago. He is remembered for his heroism in turning aside the tide of darkness during the Long Night, a legendary winter that lasted an entire generation. In order to complete the making of his sword, so the legend goes, Azor Ahai plunged the sword into the heart of his wife, Nissa Nissa (*Clash* 10, Davos 1). Thus Lightbringer was forged, the "Red Sword of Heroes." The practice of human sacrifice by R'hllor's religious adherents goes back a long way. It's something of a family tradition. The underlying hope of this tradition is that Azor Ahai will be reborn to defeat the Great Other once and for all. Arguably, the greatest power that the followers of R'hllor have is in convincing people that this prophecy is true.

It is possible that the supernatural abilities of R'hllor's priests and priestesses are connected in some way to dragon magic. It is said that Azor Ahai will return after a long summer and wake dragons out of stone. While we should be careful not to follow any prophetic hint too closely, it does seem clear that the champion will have some role in the reemergence of dragons, or vice versa. Dragons, of course, return with Dany's funeral pyre party trick. After this event, both Thoros and Melisandre are shown to wield magic beyond their full control and comprehension. It is possible that their power (or the extent of the miraculous feats they perform) is related to the reemergence of dragons. The obvious analogs here are the parallel powers of the warlocks of Qarth and the Alchemists' ability to produce wildfire. Both forms of magic are said to be enhanced following the return of dragons.

Having the right sort of royal blood might win you the support of R'hllor's priests. Being royalty will bring you popularity in the religion. And for a while, you'll be hot stuff. They may prop you up as a key player on R'hllor's chessboard. It is far more likely, however, that they will want to burn you at the stake. In this way, Martin plays with the old but common political myth that certain kinds of blood are noble. From this particular religious view, kingly blood is endowed with magical potential. If offered in the form of human sacrifice, such blood may bring divine favor to a particular army or imbue a priest with miraculous ability.

So R'hllor represents a divine power with real-world impact. It is unclear whether R'hllor is a god or a monster or some unthinking elemental force. Whatever the case, the religion is not simple superstition. Priestly mediators of R'hllor resurrect key characters. Visions of the future portend battles and motivate wartime decisions. Phantom uterus assassins made of shadow are real. But while the power wielded by these priestly mediators is undeniable, R'hllor is something of a dead-beat dad. He's out there—indeed a healthy fear of him is warranted—but his children can't count on him to provide or even visit during appropriate hours. This fire god is either hopelessly fickle or unaware.

It is therefore debatable whether or not R'hllor is intelligent and personal. Does R'hllor really desire the human sacrifices offered to him? Has he really preordained a warrior-king who will ascend to the throne? Or have R'hllor's followers simply tapped some real (albeit mindless) cosmic power and built a religion around it? These questions remain unanswered in the story.

One clue to Martin's vision might be found in his title: *A Song of Ice and Fire*. The emphasis on these two elements suggests that the religion of R'hllor—the god most associated with fire—is one of two major forces contending for supremacy. This binary vision would seem to fit within the religious beliefs of R'hllor's worshippers. Within this system, the Lord of Light (and fire) supports a few of our more heroic characters, whereas the Great Other (of darkness and ice) supports the Night King and his undead army. R'hllor is the *heart of fire* and the Great Other is the *soul of ice*.

Deep Dive: Full of Terrors

Or consider a slightly different take on Melisandre's binary mythos. In a vision, she sees Brynden "Bloodraven" Rivers—who is as much tree as man—with Bran Stark at his side. She hears the voice of Bloodraven instructing the boy, telling him to reach into the darkness like a tree sinks roots into deep earth. While readers will recognize Bloodraven and Bran as greenseers, Melisandre imagines that the man with a wooden face and a thousand red eyes is the Great Other's evil champion (*Dance* 31, Melisandre I). Clearly, the Red Priestess doesn't have enough information to distinguish the motives of the greenseers from the Others (who are themselves at war). It is Melisandre's limited perspective that makes her certainty unconscionable. More than once, Martin places her in a dialogue where she must defend her errant visionary advice. So maybe there is no R'hllor. Maybe magic is just a by-product of dragons and the folks of Asshai have developed rituals around powers they don't understand.

Here is another complication: a simplistic focus of ice-and-fire powers leaves far too many important characters and plot points out of the equation. Aside from

23. "George R. R. Martin: The World of Ice and Fire," YouTube video, 1:31:43, interview with 92nd Street Y, published October 27, 2014.

24. A date of ca. 600 BCE is sometimes given, but this date is disputed.

Great Thralls of Fire: The Religion of R'hllor

the greenseers, what of the magic of wargs and warlocks? What of the magic of the Faceless Men? The evident power of these shamans, mages, and assassins proves there is more to their beliefs than valueless fables. But from the perspective of R'hllor's religion, the binary categories of light and dark are all that matter.

This binary nature of light vs. dark might remind us, again, of *Star Wars*. Indeed, not only will our hero wield a sword of light, the great enemy is a cosmic Dark Side nemesis. While *Star Wars* is a fun analogy, we should not discount the affinities between R'hllor's religion and Zoroastrianism (also called Mazdayasna). Martin claims to have been inspired, to some extent, by this ancient Indo-Iranian faith.[23] Zoroastrianism features a singular deity and an evil, divine counterpart. The symbol of fire and a belief in an end-times savior also figure prominently in Zoroastrianism.

❧ Excursus: Zoroastrianism ❧

Zoroastrianism took shape as a distinct belief system in the teachings of a prophet named Zarathustra (a.k.a. Zoroaster) sometime before 900 BCE. But many place the prophet much earlier, perhaps as far back as 1,700 BCE in the region we now associate with modern Iran.[24] Against the backdrop of a largely polytheistic world, Zoroaster taught that only one God is worthy of worship. Zarathustra's god was Ahura Mazda, meaning the "Wise Lord." But there was a second (evil) deity, Angra Mainyu, meaning "Mind of Destruction" or "Chaotic Spirit." Angra Mainyu was associated with deception, darkness, disorder, and an unprincipled life, while Ahura Mazda was associated with light, order, and principled life.[25]

Although the idea of a messiah evolved later in the life of Zoroastrianism, some ancient texts refer to a Saoshyant, or "one who brings benefit." In Zoroastrian thought, Saoshyant evolves into a savior figure who will ultimately defeat the darkness in the last days. Basic elemental symbols, like fire and water, are important for Zoroastrianism to represent a purified life. For example, Zoroastrian "fire temples" today (e.g., in India and the United States) preserve perpetual fires. These fires are stoked five times a day. While Zoroastrianism is now one of the smaller modern religions (with approx. 200K adherents), it is one of the oldest that continues to be practiced.

25. Zoroastrianism, therefore, represents a belief system that includes good and evil deities that foreshadows many modern, popular notions of cosmic binaries (like God and Satan).

Even so, Martin's conception of R'hllor is far too sinister to draw a one-to-one correlation to Zoroastrianism. The Wise Lord of Zoroaster (Ahura Mazda) is portrayed as a uniquely good deity. Adherents of this religion preach that good thoughts, good words, and good actions lead to a peaceful society. By contrast, many of the followers of R'hllor are deceptive, power-seeking, and violent. So while Martin may have been inspired by this ancient religion, he clearly envisions the worshippers of R'hllor in a different light.

HISTORICAL BACKDROP:
SAVORY SACRIFICE

Great Thralls of Fire:
The Religion of R'hllor

MOST PEOPLE AGREE that there's nothing quite as appetizing as burning flesh. It's tasty and savory and it comes in all forms! Burning flesh can smoke, crackle, and drip with juicy animal fat. If it's lobster—as a bonus for music lovers—it just might sing to you as it boils. When it's slabs of barbecued bovine flesh, you might invite family and friends to stand around the grill and smell it before you eat it together. If so, gentle reader, you are just like many ancient sky gods.

Many ancient cultures believed that the gods were super jazzed about barbecue. Whether you're a Celt in Europe, a Talensi in Ghana, or a Mayan in South America, chances are that your god likes a good burnt offering. So when the smoke rises to the heavens (assuming that you've got the recipe right) it's going to please your god.

In the same way that your family and friends like to eat together on special occasions, ancient people wanted to commune with the gods, too. Inviting the gods to the party often meant tempting their tummies. Sometimes the offering was an entire animal burnt to a crisp (i.e., the priests gave the whole thing as a god-gift). Other times it was a community affair where the priests and people shared the food.

For the ancient mind, offering the gods food meant transforming it. The animal—via smoke—is transformed from its worldly form into a transcendent state, allowing the god to receive it. In other words, burning the animal sent the gift upward. In Hebrew, the word for burnt offering (עלה) literally means an "ascending" sacrifice.

The Israelites, however, had strict instructions for the blood of the animal. "Only be sure that you do not eat the blood; for the blood is the life, and you shall not eat the life with the meat" (Deuteronomy 12:23). The blood was believed to be the life force of the animal. The blood had special properties and required special treatment. And the Israelites were not alone in this belief. Several ancient cultures took the care of animal and human blood very seriously.

Aztec Human Sacrifice: 16th-century illustration from Codex Magliabechiano (folio 70r). In this ritual, the heart was removed from the body. The Aztecs believed that the human heart contained a fragment of the sun's heat. By removing the heart, it could be reunited with the sun. Courtesy of Wikimedia Commons.

Human sacrifice builds from the same conceptual world but emphasizes an important feature. *The gift offered to the god must be the best you have to offer.* (Don't give your dad the stale candy corn and keep all of the Reese's to yourself, kid.) There is evidence of human sacrifice in ancient cultures from the ancient Near East to sub-Saharan Africa, to Southeast Asia, to Northern Europe, to South America, etc.

The Incas, for example, believed that Viracocha (the supreme creator) was the giver of all life. Human sacrifice was a way to give a token of the gift of life back to the Father. Of course, if you're going to give your very best gift, you'll be sending a few people you love back to Viracocha. This means children. But it would only be children without any observable blemish. It had to be the cutest kids in all of the land and these children were sometimes dressed as royalty for the big day. It's sort of like if modern folks sent all of our favorite child actors to the mountains and never saw them again (RIP Gary Coleman). The Incan practice of *Qhapaq hucha* can be translated as "royal obligation."

It seems that Martin has created the rituals of R'hllor by piecing together several different ancient beliefs. Like most gods, R'hllor communes with his people during sacrificial offerings and listens to their requests in this context (at least, this is what Melisandre thinks). But Martin adds the wrinkle about blood magic. In this case, royal blood is especially effective in getting R'hllor's attention. For most cultures that practiced ritual sacrifice, however, a child with a notable skin blemish (e.g., Shireen Baratheon) wouldn't be selected for offering.

CHARACTER STUDY: THOROS OF MYR

WHILE IT'S TRUE that the followers of R'hllor tend to be overconfident about their religion, Thoros of Myr is the exception. Thoros was decisively brazen as a warrior, but brazenly indecisive as a priest—so much so that for a time he shrugs off his duties in Robert Baratheon's court and becomes the king's party pal. Thoros slips into doubt about the religion of R'hllor and spends his days drinking and kicking ass in the tournament *mêlée*. He becomes known in King's Landing for his fiery sword (not a metaphor for gonorrhea; he actually sets his blade ablaze), for being slovenly dressed, drunk, and rotund. If we can put the HBO depiction of him aside, Thoros is the Lebowskian "Dude" of Westeros.[26]

Character Study: Thoros of Myr

Thoros joins Beric Dondarrion in his attempt to arrest Gregor Clegane (a nihilist of sorts), who is terrorizing the Riverlands. To the chagrin of the Starks, Ser Gregor "the Mountain" cannot be brought to justice. Beric's posse is caught by surprise and overmatched at Mummer's Ford. Beric is impaled by the Mountain's spear. His untimely death is the precursor for what Pulp Fiction's Jules would call an "according-to-Hoyle miracle."

Acting as a priest of R'hllor—although a dubious and drunken priest—Thoros performs the last rites for Beric. This involves what is called the "kiss of life" in Essos. By breathing fire into the mouth of Beric, Thoros enacts a symbolic purification of his dead commander. This fiery French kiss results in the resurrection of Beric and—to an extent—the reviving of Thoros' faith. Thoros is shocked by the resurrection, as he only intended the ritual as religious symbol. Knowing that the miracle cannot be explained by his own piety (indeed, he has none), Thoros attributes the miracle to R'hllor. He doesn't claim to know why R'hllor has intervened, but he no longer doubts that R'hllor got involved. Moreover, the miracle is repeatable: Thoros raises Beric from the dead multiple times.

This event casts Thoros almost as a St. Paul type. Famously, Paul (better called Saul) witnessed the resur-

26. This, of course, makes Robert Baratheon a hybrid of Walter and King Ralph. Although we guess that Bobby B. would roll on Shabbos if indeed the *mêlée* could not be rescheduled.

rected Christ while on the road to Damascus and reignited his native faith. So for both Thoros and Paul, resurrection sparked their faith. Or perhaps an analogy with Constantine is warranted. As the Christian historian Eusebius explains, Constantine received a vision from Christ before the battle of the Milvian Bridge and adopted the sign of the cross for his army. This analogy, while not perfect, draws a parallel between Constantine and Thoros as warriors who begin crusades. Whether or not Martin had either Paul or Constantine in mind, his portrayal of Thoros reminds us of two realities in the ancient world.

The Staffordshire Hoard: The Staffordshire hoard is a cache of ca. 7th-century items, including several precious metals used to adorn weapons. The golden band pictured in the lower left-hand side of the photograph shows the marriage of warfare and sacred scripture. This band is engraved with Numbers 10:35, which reads: "Arise, O Lord, let your enemies be scattered, and your foes flee before you." Courtesy of Wikimedia Commons.

First, faith was not a given in the ancient or medieval world. It often took the perception of a miracle to ignite faith. Second, divine intervention is often linked to warfare in the ancient and medieval periods.

For the Christian historian Eusebius, the story of Constantine's vision provided a plausible explanation for a military victory and a new era in Roman history. In Martin's world, the miracle of Beric's resurrection leads to the establishment of the Brotherhood Without Banners. Thoros is both priest and warrior within this army. From a medieval perspective, there is no necessary distinction between religion and war.

This band of outlaws will eventually be fortified by a new leader: Lady Stoneheart. She—animated by the life force of Beric—returns to avenge her lost family. This key plot point is only made possible by the reluctant but ritually potent Thoros of Myr.

FAN THEORY FUN: FIERY FUGAZI

YOU WOULD BE hard-pressed to find a fan who believes that the Seven Gods of Westeros represent real deities. Most fans, it seems, are of the opinion at the Faith of the Seven is a political construct without any supernatural foundation. But the same cannot be said of R'hllor's religion. Say what you will of Melisandre's misplaced certainty, but she's pretty good at killing dudes with her religious rigmarole.[27] Parlaying this into a nice little logical formula isn't difficult:

Premise 1: Melisandre demonstrates real power.

Premise 2: Melisandre credits real R'hllor for her real power.

Conclusion: R'hllor is real.

27. For this line of thought, see Reece, "Why Doesn't Everyone Believe in R'hllor?," the Wood between Worlds (blog), June 4, 2013. Reece (among others) suggests that R'hllor is real, albeit evil.

The leap here is in the assumption that Melisandre knows what she's talking about. Several fans have pointed out that we've seen no proof of R'hllor as a divine agent. The Lord of Light, so says this theory, is just as fraudulent as the Seven. If so, we should draw a distinction between blood magic and the religion that is constructed around it. Generally speaking, Melisandre has some facility with magic but cannot be trusted to interpret its source or ultimate outcomes.[28]

28. Compare, for example, the comments by "Drowned Priest," on A Forum of Ice and Fire (fan forum), April 10, 2012. Earlier breadcrumbs of this theory might be traced to "devotee," November 19, 2008. The second of these suggested the possibility that Melisandre would lose her faith (to some degree) toward the end of her character arc. This seems to be something that the showrunners are playing with.

Most proponents of this theory are *not* saying that Melisandre's power is just party tricks and placebo effects. Clearly, Martin's world contains the possibility of magic. But these fans are quick to point out the fallacy that a divine personality is the best explanation for it. After all, several practitioners of magic exist in this world, and only a few appeal to R'hllor. Thus the religious interpretation of blood magic is arbitrary.

So is the Lord of Light really real? Or is he a fiery fugazi? We are unlikely to get a definitive answer from the narrative or the show. Martin has said that no gods are likely to show up in the story (any more than they already do).[29] This, as with so many fan debates, will remain unsolved.

29. Charlie Jane Anders, "George R. R. Martin Explains Why We'll Never Meet Any Gods in A Song of Ice and Fire," io9.com, July 21, 2011.

BIRD'S-EYE VIEW: MARTIN'S MONOTHEISM

C LASSICAL THEISM IS the belief that there is a supreme being. This being is the creator and therefore transcendent. But this creator also intervenes at times in human affairs. Theism is usually associated with Western world religions. It is often contrasted with pantheism (the universe is God), animism (certain spirits animate parts of nature), or modern atheism (no god). There are other kinds of theism in metaphysical debates, but Christianity and Islam are the most practiced forms of theism worldwide. Both are considered "Western" by academics (due to the geography of their first adherents, not because of where they are practiced today).

Bird's-Eye View: Martin's Monotheism

George R. R. Martin has a tendency to cast religions that we might associate with Western theism in a negative light. This is not always the case. But the fact that Melisandre is burning people at the stake in service to her Red God isn't a good look. No character in his world is entirely ethical or evil. But we are far more likely to find evil cultists than Mother Teresa types. With this in mind, Melisandre is introduced to the narrative antagonistically (although her narrative arc remains uncertain). We could say the same for most worshippers of the Drowned God and the God of Death (both theistic rather than animistic).

This doesn't necessarily mean that Martin intends an indictment of Christianity, Judaism, Islam, or Zoroastrianism. It is more likely that Martin utilizes these religions to create needed plot points. For a writer of high fantasy, Martin brings an unusually high degree of realism into his religious and political institutions. And what better way to achieve authenticity than to borrow heavily from various historical religions? In his world, political conflict is necessary; indeed political maneuvering is integral to the plot. In order to provide nuance and variance, Martin uses religious zealots and religious power structures as literary devices. Some characters are motivated by greed, others seek revenge, and some—like the Blues Brothers—are on a mission from God. *A Song of Ice and Fire*, however, isn't a slapstick comedy. So it is natural that the missional characters in Martin's story are entangled, impure, and (more often than not) evil.

This brings us, as readers, to a most delicious discomfort. Almost no character is pure in Martin's world. Every character that matters is tainted by vices or moral deficits in some way. But we invest in—indeed, we root for—some evils more than others. Part of Martin's magic is to get us to love killers like Arya, the Hound, and Tyrion. For better or worse, very few of Martin's most beloved sinners are entrenched within theistic religion.

House Rules

FATHERS, KINGS, AND GODS

3

*It is society which, fashioning us in its image, fills us with
religious, political and moral beliefs that control our actions.*

—ÉMILE DURKHEIM

Distinctive Elements

- ❧ honor and duty
- ❧ encoded collectivism
- ❧ overuse of the term "bastard"

Key Adherents

- ❧ Robb Stark
- ❧ Tywin Lannister
- ❧ pretty much everyone else

TRAVEL GUIDE

ARE YOU BORED with the usual holiday hotspots?
Tired of the same old sandy beaches at sunset?
There comes a point in every seasoned traveler's
life when a new horizon must be explored. So if you're
a wealthy, well-connected, and generally fortunate
fellow, allow yourself to be tempted by a bit of Westerosi
wanderlust! Men of means will enjoy harassing servants
and murdering butcher's boys without consequence. If,
however, you are not a man of means . . . well, Westeros
is going to totally suck for you. It will probably result in
your grisly, meaningless death. But the tapestries can be
quite lovely.

There is perhaps no better location for cultural nostalgia than King's Landing. The Great Sept of Baelor, the Red Keep, and the Iron Throne will remind you of simpler times (when homicide detectives lacked forensic science). Visit Oldtown, home of the greatest library in the Seven Kingdoms (women and children not admitted). If sun and sand is your thing, the people of Dorne will probably not poison you (sometimes it's the scorpions or vipers). Enjoy the surf and serfdom of the Iron Islands (no lifeguard on duty). The kiddos will enjoy petting direwolf pups near Winterfell (and the severed heads of craven deserters). Westeros truly has something for everyone!

House Rules:
Fathers, Kings, and Gods

DEEP DIVE:
HOMO DADPLEX

IF GEORGE R. R. Martin's epic is a chess match, the opening moves pit the Starks against the Lannisters. It would be a mistake to think of Martin's world as black and white. But the Starks are generally more beholden to honor, duty, and tradition. They are not generally known for their intrigue or political savvy. The Lannisters are almost a mirror opposite. Tywin Lannister is known primarily for his good credit score and for defecating precious metal. This, of course, is a good reputation to promote if indeed one is a rising family with high political aspirations. Ned Stark, by contrast, fathers one of the oldest families in Westeros and, as such, is beholden to the status quo. Hence honor, duty, and tradition. Ned may indeed be a savvy field commander, but he is better known for his redundant weather forecasts.

Some fans have argued, moreover, that Ned Stark suffers from numpty-brain. (Numpty-brain is the rare condition that comes from being both stupid and British at the same time.)[30] By contrast, Tywin demonstrates a brilliance that very few possess. He is known for his ability to acquire and maintain power even when honor, duty, and tradition demand otherwise.

What both lords have in common is an awareness of their own mortality and the priority each places on his family's well-being. If so, we would argue that Tywin places his children in a better position for success at the time of his departure, whereas Ned leaves his family and house in chaos. Or rendered more simply: numpty-brain.

It should be said, however, that both men die in shame and Ned's quick departure might be a better way to go. (Tywin meets his fate in the privy chamber. Here we have a possible echo of the very nonfictional Edmund Ironside, who found a knife-wielding knave waiting under his toilet [ca. 1016].[31] Other accounts of this story suggest that Edmund's demise was met with a crossbow.) Martin's world does sometimes reward political savvy but no character outwits the god of death. The best you can do is delay the inevitable by saying "not today."

In general, the reputations of Tywin and Ned are more true than false and speak to their respective values. Each was respected in his own way and each passed on his values to his children. In short, these two families have been socialized differently.

Émile Durkheim—celebrated as the father of modern social science—would love the Starks. Ned, Catelyn, Sansa, Benjen, and especially Jon Snow would be of great interest to Durkheim as examples of religious sociology (although the Starks would only be one example in Martin's world). These characters model what sociologists call *homo duplex.*

Durkheim argued that we humans (*homo*) are creatures with two levels (*duplex*). Our primary level is

30. See "numpty," Scottish informal (slang), *Collins English Dictionary,* collinsdictionary.com.

Deep Dive:
Homo Dadplex

31. See Henry of Huntingdon, *The History of the English People, 1000–1154,* trans. Diana Greenway (Oxford: Oxford University Press, 2002), 15. Unlike Tywin, however, it was another man's son who played the *Scheißkerl.*

32. Émile Durkheim, *The Elementary Forms of Religious Life*, trans. Karen E. Fields, reprint ed. (New York: Free Press, 1995).

33. Durkheim, *Elementary Forms*, 44. Durkheim did not come to this view until the latter part of his career. In his earlier writings, he was uninterested in religion.

34. Yuval Noah Harari, *Sapiens: A Brief History of Humankind* (London: Harvill Secker, 2014).

instinctual. We seek food, water, shelter, defend ourselves against immediate threats and try our best to procreate (or rehearse the activity). At our most basic, we are quite a bit like other animals.[32]

We are, however, capable of a second level of consciousness: the religious level. For Durkheim, religion is a social reality, indeed the most basic human institution. Religion is constructed of the "beliefs and practices which unite in one single moral community."[33] The uniquely human ability to band together in large groups around abstract ideas is at the same time "religious" and the beginnings of society.

Or, to borrow from a more recent theorist, we Homo Sapiens outpace our animal relatives when we begin to put words to abstract concepts. Birds and monkeys can warn each other about lions. But only an animal capable of inventing abstract ideas can tell stories about wolf-spirit guides and build tribes around such ideas. The ability to make myths fits hand-in-glove with religion and—most importantly—fits hand-in-glove with social order.[34]

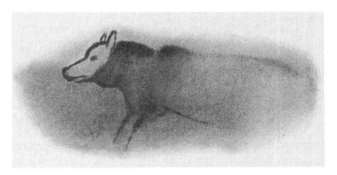

Prehistoric Wolf Painting: The Font de Gaume cavern in southwest France preserves several paintings and engravings over 10,000 years old. Courtesy of Wikimedia Commons.

Humans have the ability to create communities of thousands and millions around myths (e.g., *Star Wars*) or abstract ideas (e.g., democratic capitalism). The invention of religious myth is a very early and necessary step in what Yuval Harari calls the "cognitive revolution."

Most importantly, for Durkheim, religion—the higher level of *homo duplex*—is how a society encodes compassion into otherwise self-invested creatures. The higher level of *homo duplex* is where we hold our primal instincts at bay and consider the collective well-being of society. It is also worth pointing out that, from this perspective, communities formed around the Grateful Dead or *Star Trek* could be considered "religious."

So why would Durkheim love the Starks? It's not the sacred trees (although these are integral) and it's not the rituals (however important); the most crucial "religious" aspect of House Stark is its social code. The Starks are an example of a community with encoded morals and taboos. Take as case in point the social force of "guest right" ideology, with all of its related duties, mythology, and restrictions.

In a world where murder is often the easiest way to solve one's problems, we might ask: why doesn't the social order fall into complete chaos? Why does anyone—much less multiple mentors—help Arya? Why does Tyrion care for bastards and broken things? Why is Daenerys hell-bent on ending slavery? If winter is coming, why don't more Northerners eat the weak among them? The answer is that societies (both ancient and modern) construct bulwarks against total chaos. Think about all of the restrictions on murder in Martin's world: folks frown upon kingslaying, kinslaying, cannibalism, and killing children. Using lethal poison is belittled as feminine and most women aren't

Deep Dive: Homo Dadplex

allowed to be warriors. *With all of these restrictions on murder, how does any murdering get done at all?*

House Rules:
Fathers, Kings, and Gods

"Guest right" is the parade example of a social bulwark (i.e., Durkheim's notion of religion). The practice of protecting a guest beneath one's roof is among the most honored religious traditions in Martin's world. It is especially sacred in the North and violating it is an evil met with the harshest of penalties (*World*, "The North"). In sum, host and guest are not supposed to kill each other— like, at all. Not even if one guy is really hungry and the other guy is especially succulent. Even if you're feeling super murdery, you're just *not* supposed to kill that guy.

The ritual of eating together (bread and salt) and the divine mandate associated with it (old gods and new) reinforce the taboo. The practice is also encoded in a story told to children about a cook who becomes a giant rat. The cook angers the gods by killing and cooking a king's son into a pie (*Storm* 56, Bran IV). Explicit in every telling of the story is the moral that ties the will of the gods to sacred nature of guest right.

☙ Excursus: Zeus ❧

Zeus' prominence in Greek mythology is demonstrated by his many titles. Zeus is the ruler of the skies, king of the gods, and the god of heaven (located on Mt. Olympus). The Roman god Jupiter was modeled after him. He also shares several characteristics with the Norse god Odin. Zeus is also called the father of gods and men. Given how promiscuous he was, his status as "father" was both figurative and biological.

> In keeping with his role as a father, Zeus was thought to be a provider and protector, caring especially for the poor (when he wasn't busy hurling lightning at liars and being a shape-shifting rapist). He was also called "Zeus Hospites" and "Zeus Xenios." Both titles associate him with hospitality, especially for impoverished pilgrims. So among all of his other duties, he also functioned as the god of guest right. Wealthy men who feared Zeus would offer room and protection to pilgrims.

Deep Dive: Homo Dadplex

Perhaps even more fundamental than guest right is the system of tribal ethics and social relationships encoded in sons, fathers, lords, and kings. The next step in this patriarchy, of course, is gods. The lines between ancestors, kings, and gods are blurred in many ancient cultures. Because these were often overlapping categories, devotion to a mortal father figure was often infused with divine significance.

So we suggest a variation to Durkheim's *homo duplex*. We call it *homo dadplex*, because the communal function of religion and its moral character are entangled with patriarchy. To be "religious" in the ancient world was to honor the sons, fathers, lords, kings, and gods.[35]

Conversely, a father figure's honor depended on his ability to care for the tribe. He was the face of the tribe to outsiders, made decisions related to farming, defense, arranged marriages, etc.[36] If he—whether a father, lord, or king—failed to care for his tribe, he would answer to the gods. So too in Martin's world: devotion to one's liege lord is nothing less than sacred. Or put more simply: homo dadplex.

35. Scholars now question whether "religion" is the right word to use for ancient peoples. But in this case we're nuancing Durkheim, who saw no problem with applying the category of religion to ancient practices of ritual, worship, and the sacred.

36. The Romans called this office *paterfamilias*, meaning "father of the family." But the dynamic translation "Lord of the House" describes the office better.

Robert Baratheon, when set against this backdrop, is altogether unethical. Robert's lack of care for those in his service makes him fiscally and morally bankrupt. He refuses to manage his wealth with integrity, thus weakening the power of the throne. He's a deadbeat dad to his eldest son, thus weakening the kingdom. It is no coincidence that his favorite phrase is "seven hells!" No doubt he plans to visit all of them.

Within Martin's world, a far more pious phrase would be *I love it when you call me Big Papa.* Because to wear the B.I.G. crown, sweetie, you've got to feed the needy. By this standard, someone like Tywin Lannister is a far more ethical father figure. His emotional availability notwithstanding, he provides for those in care, he prepares his eldest son to lead, he defends his tribe, and he reinforces the social system. Tywin would be a colossal failure as a father in modern society; but he is something close to the ideal father against Martin's feudal backdrop. This fact ought to caution us against any nostalgia for "simpler times."

Returning to sociology, we should recognize that Westerosi society is a form of collectivism. In contrast to modern individualism, collectivist cultures tend to have tribal ethics. Think about the difference between these two questions:

1. The ethical individualist asks: what's the right thing to do?

2. The ethical collectivist asks: *what's the right thing to do for my tribe?*

The first question assumes some kind of universal standard for right and wrong. In this worldview, a person must live up to the standard. The second assumes that the tribe's overall well-being determines a person's actions. To philosophy nerds, this may sound like consequentialism (which argues that the best outcome for the most people determines ethical choice), but remember that Martin's world is fundamentally tribal. As such, the strength of the father and eldest son is crucial for the tribe.

This is why Jaime Lannister is infinitely more important to Tywin than his other children. This is why Randyll Tarly banishes his eldest son (a self-confessed coward) to a life of monastic servitude. These examples show the dark side of *homo dadplex*. If your personal well-being is contrary to the well-being of the tribe, you get no chocolate. You get nothing. You lose. Good day, sir.

So Arya can't be a knight and Tyrion can't be a liege lord. Daenerys is a child bride and Loras is expected to sire children.[37] *Homo dadplex* can be especially hazardous to personal identity. At the same time, it functions as a bulwark against total chaos. Tribes function as tribes for a reason.

Tribes can also be beautiful, providing a meaningful existence and teaching compassion. For all of the darkness explored by Martin, we meet characters encoded with compassion. After all, once a person is taught compassion *by the tribe*, that person may choose to show compassion *outside of the tribe*. In Martin's world, we get to see some characters discover moral alternatives to *homo dadplex*.

Deep Dive: Homo Dadplex

37. It is noteworthy that in Martin's world noble women often reinforce the patriarchy. For example, Catelyn pressures Ned to answer his king's call to serve as Hand (book only; *Game* 6, Catelyn 11). She also supports Robb as king and loathes Jon Snow, who (to her knowledge) is an outsider to the tribal structure. Or consider Brienne of Tarth, who is willing to defend her king and die for him if necessary. Brienne's devotion to House Stark also reinforces the system even if she only fits within it uncomfortably.

HISTORICAL BACKDROP: WHAT'S IN A SIGIL?

WHEN THE ALWAYS astute and self-aware Lady Olenna tells you which sigils follow the *rule of cool*, take note. She, of House Tyrell, tells us that a banner featuring a golden rose doesn't elicit much respect. Direwolves and krakens are far better for battlefield use (S03E04, "And Now His Watch Has Ended"). As usual, Lady Olenna is right. The clans you have to look out for in Martin's world are well represented. The Northern houses are especially known for their ferocious sigils: a bull moose, a silver fist, a roaring giant, a black bear, just to name a few. The bottom line with sigils is power.

In the medieval world, a sigil was a device imbued with power. Sigillary banners were more than mascots; they're dynamos of thaumaturgy.[38] Martin—as is his way—borrows from this concept and gives it a fantasy upgrade. The direwolf of House Stark is a case in point: this sigil bespeaks the special power of the Starks. It is then literally embodied on the battlefield in the form of Grey Wind and the (forever) Young Wolf. But regardless of whether your sigil is a magical beast or an intimidating concept, it ought to capture the life force of your house.

So what's up with House Bolton? The Boltons' sigil is a flayed human body against a pink field, patterned with red drops of blood. Rather than embracing some fierce predator or warrior, these Dreadfort devils boast of their tortured victims. And in case you missed the point, the Bolton words get right to it: "Our Blades Are Sharp." If the *Flayed Man* doesn't follow the *rule of cool*, it at least follows the rule of cruel.

Yes, "Our Blades Are Sharp" lacks subtlety. Yes, a man without skin (except Eddie from Iron Maiden) is in poor taste. And, yes, red against pink is a frightful color scheme. But no, this is not one of those times when Martin's world is any stranger than ours. It may seem grotesque at first glance to embrace a symbol of torture and to imbue it with supernatural power. But is it any less grotesque than a crucifix?

Famously, Emperor Constantine embraced the cross of Christ as his sigil after the battle of the Milvian Bridge (312 CE). What was once a symbol of Roman torture

38. From the Greek *thauma*, meaning "miracle" or "marvel" and ergon, meaning "work." It usually describes a form of magic that effects change in the physical world.

would become a sigil of Roman Christianity. While the standard t-shaped cross is either religious or banal in the modern world, the cross was a symbol of terror in the ancient world. It is also safe to say that the symbol continued to terrorize the enemies of European Christianity in the centuries of the crusades. According to legend (Eusebius' second account), Constantine received a vision of a cross and these words: "In this sign, conquer" (ἐν τούτῳ νίκα). Arguably, this is exactly what Christianity did over the next millennia. The cross is now featured on the national flags of Denmark, England, Finland, Georgia, Iceland, Norway, Sweden, Switzerland, Tonga, etc. All of these countries, for what it's worth, abide by the Geneva Conventions (condemning torture).

Historical Backdrop: What's in a Sigil?

The Crucifixion of Saint Andrew: 17th-century oil on canvas. Artist unknown. Courtesy of Wikimedia Commons.

75

There may be an echo of cruciform sigils in the HBO depiction of House Bolton's sigil. On screen, the *Flayed Man* is hung on an X-shaped cross (while Jesus made the t-shaped cross famous, the Romans employed crosses of different shapes). Could this be a nod to the X-shaped cross (or "saltire") of Scotland? According to legend, St. Andrew—disciple of Jesus, turned patron saint—refused to be martyred in the same manner as his master. So old Andrew was hung up like Theon in the Dreadfort rumpus room.

This is where the similarities between the Boltons and the fine people of Scotland end (except for all the other parallels). Our point here is simply to suggest that torture sigils were very much at home in the medieval North. Moreover, they have an especially religious history.

CHARACTER STUDY:
ROBB STARK

BELYING THE GRAND tradition of Stark honor, Robb Stark meets his downfall after a king-sized falsehood. Robb is both strong and clever beyond his years as a battle commander. Like his father, he's beholden to tradition.[39] Robb's bannermen respect him. His baby-blue eyes are swoon-worthy in both the show and the books (*Game* 1, Bran I). And he's got a direwolf who thinks that Umbers are finger-lickin' good (Game 53, Bran VI). By all measures, Robb is the perfect *KINGA DA NORF!*

Robb's one and only defeat unfolds in a southern dining hall (House Frey is located just south of the Neck). After agreeing to an arranged marriage to one of Walder Frey's daughters, Robb breaks his vow and weds Talisa Maegyr (or Jeyne Westerling, for book purists). He eventually apologizes and begs forgiveness from Lord Frey—but

39. See, for example, his confrontational reception of Tyrion. Robb meets him seated, with unsheathed sword resting on his knees. This is the proper, lordly way to refuse guest right. Clearly he takes the custom seriously. (*Game* 24, Bran IV.)

he doesn't repent. He remains married to Talisa, who is now pregnant with his child. The Freys feign forgiveness and even grant the Starks guest right under their roof. Walder Frey appeals to the Andal gods in his welcome as he offers them protection in the "light of the Seven" (S03E09, "The Rains of Castamere"). Yada, yada . . . blood everywhere.

Character Study: Robb Stark

☙ Excursus: Medieval Romance ❧

In the medieval world, romantic courtship was not completely unknown. Persian love poetry had a profound impact on noblemen and ladies at court circa (probably before) 1100 CE. Troubadours popularized love songs featuring brave heroes who wooed wealthy ladies. In other words, French and Italian singers borrowed the theme from Persian poetry and put a European spin on it.

As a result, the tradition of arranged marriage began to fall out of fashion in the West. It would take centuries for romance-motivated marriage to become commonplace and even longer for it to become commonsense. The term *romanz* in Old French means "verse narrative." The term was not used in the sense of generic eroticism until much later.[40]

---

40. For more, see Le Donne, "From Persia, with Love," ch. 6 in *The Wife of Jesus: Ancient Texts and Modern Scandals* (London: Oneworld, 2015).

Robb's miscalculation is catastrophic. With this single massacre, Walder Frey is able to end the Northern rebellion, strengthen his ties with the Iron Throne and Casterly Rock, and deliver the North to Roose Bolton. The fact that Walder is able to get revenge for Robb's broken promise is icing on the cake. Now consider what Robb lost: his kingship, his new bride, his unborn child, several of his bannermen, and his life. Eclipsing all of these losses is this: his mistake allowed the Boltons (longtime rivals to the Starks) to take the North.

Given the significance of this event for the overall plot, we must ask: *how and why did Robb fail so miserably?* We think that Robb's miscalculation was underpinned by a religious misunderstanding. Crucial here is the religious difference between North and South.

According to the *World of Ice & Fire*, Northmen hold the custom of guest right dearer than any other; the Andals (most of the families south of the Neck) honored something like guest right, "but it looms less large in southron minds" (*World,* "The North"). This is not to say that the southern folk are less religious. Look no further than their religious devotion to trial by combat. But the devotion to guest right functions differently and with more core value in Northern religion. To use Durkheim's concept, guest right has been encoded into the descendants of the First Men; it is integral to their *homo duplex.*

Robb knows that he has broken an important vow to Walder Frey. Robb knows that Frey is mean-spirited, vulgar, vindictive, and spiteful. Catelyn has warned her son that Lord Frey is dangerous. Walder's history also suggests that he's an opportunist. He is known as the "Late Walder Frey" because he heeded his liege lord's banner call at the Trident only after the outcome was no longer in doubt. But even in knowing all of this about Lord Frey, Robb still agrees to dine under his roof. *Why?*

Although Robb distrusts his host, he trusts the sacred ritual of guest right. He simply cannot fathom that Lord Frey will commit the abomination of breaking a guest-right promise. *Who would risk dishonoring their house in the eyes of the gods?* The simple answer is Walder Frey: the man who takes his vows casually and who is in no way beholden to the sacred traditions of the North.

Robb Stark's deficit, we think, isn't just a between-the-legs problem. He could have romanced Talisa and also kept his vow to House Frey. Kings are often able to manage such affairs. And while he may not share Tyrion's intellect, his problem isn't between the ears. Instead, Robb's problem is a fundamental misjudgment of religious ritual. Robb fails to appreciate the religious difference between the North and South.

Character Study: Robb Stark

FAN THEORY FUN: IS ROOSE BOLTON A VAMPIRE?

INTRIGUING FAN SPECULATION about the bloodthirsty North fuels countless hours of internet debate. Is there a dormant dragon buried at Winterfell? Does Bran Stark travel back in time to become the Night King? How many licks does it take to get to the center of Castle Black? But by far the most entertaining theory relates to super-creepy Lord Roose Bolton. How super-creepy is he? The Lord of Castle Dreadfort might even be *supernaturally* creepy. Some fans speculate that Lord Bolton is a secret vampire. This beloved theory is also known as "The Roose Is Loose," or "BOLT ON!"[41]

The Boltons are an ancient and proud house, once kings in their own right. But what if instead of the conventional medieval lineage of fathers handing down traditions and titles to sons, there has only ever been one Lord Bolton? Could he be an immortal who uses blood magic to steal the skins of his heirs and hide the fact that he never ages and never dies?

41. Primary credit goes to Redditors JBTalley and maj312.

79

Preposterous, you might say, but the theory has a lot going for it, at least on paper. It neatly explains why Roose Bolton continues to tolerate his bastard ("bastard" in every sense of the term). Even though Ramsay has murdered his legitimate heir and is a constant thorn in his side, Roose keeps him around. Ramsay's pointless cruelty runs counter to Roose's own leadership philosophy of a "peaceful land and quiet people" (*Dance* 32, Reek III). He puts up with Ramsay's psychopathic tendencies because he's raising him like a fattened calf to be slaughtered when the time is right.

Fan Theory Fun: Is Roose Bolton a Vampire?

Let's consider the strength of the evidence. Roose's age is very hard to pin down. Martin hints several times that Roose is well past forty years old (*Dance* 20, Reek II). So just how long has Roose been getting AARP magazines? A handful of clues suggest that he's forever young.

The younger sister of Roose's second wife is Barbrey Dustin, described as "still tall, unbent and handsome. She has wrinkles around her mouth and eyes, and her hair is equal parts brown and grey" (*Dance* 32, Reek III). One could assume that Roose's wife would be of a similar age, if not younger.

Roose was the Lord of the Dreadfort by his own right when Ned Stark was just a boy. Roose's first son, Domeric (murdered by Ramsay), was of a similar age to Ned's younger sister, Lyanna. If Roose is old enough to inherit his ancestral seat and father a child of Domeric's age, he'd have to be in his late forties—if not well into his fifties—during the time of *A Song of Ice and Fire*. Despite this, Theon remarks, "though Roose had been in battles, he bore no scars. Though well past forty, he was as yet unwrinkled, with scarce a line to tell of the passage of time" (*Dance* 20, Reek II). Also, according to Theon, "there was an agelessness about him, a stillness."

It is often noticed by his peers how strange it is that Roose Bolton never drinks (presumably, wine). Fans of the horror genre will remember that Dracula was also a teetotaler. Admittedly, this is a weak parallel. But keep in mind that Martin's world winks to werewolf mythology (compare the warging Stark children) and Frankenstein's monster (compare Ser Robert Strong). So a nod to Dracula isn't out of character for Martin.

While at the haunted ruins of Harrenhal, Roose obsessively searches through old tomes. Arya frequently finds him reading from the yellow pages of thick leather-bound books. After carefully reading each one, Roose burns them (*Clash* 64, Arya x). What was Roose looking for? Fans subscribing to the vampire theory suggest that he was looking for a copy of *Blood Magic for Active Seniors* (or something like it). A century before the Baratheon period, "Mad" Danelle Lothston was the Lady of Harrenhal. It was rumored that she turned to the dark arts and bathed in blood to maintain her youthful appearance.[42] On moonless nights monstrous bats flew from Harrenhal to steal children and bring them back to Mad Danelle. Could it be that Roose was searching through these grimoires to learn Lady Lothston's secrets?

Of course, we already know of types of blood magic that allow one to assume the form of other individuals. The Faceless Men of Braavos practice the ritual of applying a new face to mask their own. This ritual involves moistening the preserved skin with blood so that it seamlessly fits over one's own face. Not for nothing: the Dreadfort is proximate to Braavos, being just across the Narrow Sea at similar latitude.

Roose is also known as "the Leech Lord," after his fondness for being leeched. This is interesting on the face of it because of the reference to bloodsucking. But his

42. This may be a reference to the infamous Countess Elizabeth Báthory (Ecsedi Báthory Erzsébet) (1560–1614). Báthory was a Hungarian serial killer and probable mass-murderer. While the exact number is unknown, she was rumored to have tortured, mutilated, and murdered hundreds of girls. She was also rumored to have bathed in the blood of virgins in an attempt to preserve her youth. Our thanks to Joshua Paul Smith for this bit of blood-bath history (a.k.a. bloodbáthory).

penchant for leeching could also be explained as something to encourage circulation in the dead skins that he wears to maintain his human identity, and to prevent blood-pooling and discoloration. Indeed, leeches are still used in modern medicine to treat skin grafts and encourage circulation on amputated limbs and extremities that have been surgically reattached.

Fan Theory Fun: Is Roose Bolton a Vampire?

Now for the final nail in the coffin: the Boltons are known for their grim house sigil, the Flayed Man. This sigil is thought to be a carryover from the ancient practice of skinning captives alive. Not only are Bolton men known for this, they proudly display this fact on their banner. But what if Roose is the immortal Flayed Man? As such, Roose is raising his heirs and then using their skin and blood to change his appearance with every successive generation. With his grisly pink banners, he's been proudly advertising his supernatural scheme to hold and consolidate his power for millennia!

For all of its merit, showrunners David Benioff and D. B. Weiss neglected to follow these bread crumbs. Roose is stabbed to death by Ramsay in season 6, rudely proving himself mortal (S06E02, "Home"). But the theory remains undead for book-only fans.

BIRD'S-EYE VIEW: BOBBY WEIRWOOD

As we discussed in chapter 1, Martin has confirmed that the "old gods" of the North are loosely based on the animistic elements of Wicca and Celtic ritual.[43] Even so, the author has infused the Stark mythos with a more modern cult following: the Grateful Dead. Martin is a self-identified Deadhead and has incorporated references to their songs in previous

43. Martin, "Talks at Google," YouTube.com, August 6, 2011.

44. "George R. R. Martin: The World of Ice and Fire," YouTube.com, October 27, 2014.

45. Another example of Martin's musicology is the homage paid to saxophonist Clarence Clemens (most famous for his E Street Band membership). Clarence, a Rock & Roll Hall of Fame inductee, was nicknamed "Big Man" and played with numerous artists, including the Grateful Dead. In Martin's world, there is an eight-foot tall Ser Clarence who collected "dead heads" of wizards, priests, lords, etc. The dead heads are animated by magic, speak to Clarence, give him advice, and talk among themselves in whispers. The real-life Clarence wasn't eight feet tall, but he was 6'5"and also communed with Deadheads (*Feast* 14, Brienne III). For a medieval analog to Ser Clarence, Count Johann Ferdinand von Kufstein was rumored to have ten tiny humanoids of his own making (called "homunculi") in glass jars. According to legend, they were able to prophesy future events. See also Brocktoon.

46. Martin, "Talks at Google," YouTube.com, August 6, 2011.

books. "I have Grateful Dead lyrics always coming around and rattling around in my head."[44]

So in addition to medieval inspirations, the Stark sigil of a direwolf may well draw from the Grateful Dead song "The Dire Wolf." The lyrics of the song suggest an icy forest setting with ground frozen ten-feet deep. The dire wolf in this song—all six hundred pounds of it—is a hulking figure that arrives while the singer is sleeping. This sounds remarkably similar to the conditions of the dreaming children at Winterfell who meet their wolf-selves while sleeping.[45]

It is also possible that the sacred weirwood trees are a nod to Grateful Dead founding member Bobby Weir. But we ought not assume any one-to-one connection. Martin explains that the major religions of his world are created by combining various elements. "I take certain tenants of the religions but then I take part of this and part of that and I meld them together and I think about it and I add a few imaginative elements."[46]

We should expect, then, that the animism of Stark religion—perhaps including the Stark sigil—is an amalgam of various ruminations rattling around in Martin's (Dead) head.

Seven Hells!

SUMMA SEPTOLOGICA

4

It sounds like a fairy-tale, but not only that; this story of what man by his science and practical inventions has achieved on this earth, where he first appeared as a weakly member of the animal kingdom, and on which each individual of his species must ever again appear as a helpless infant . . . is a direct fulfillment of all, or of most, of the dearest wishes in his fairy-tales. All these possessions he has acquired through culture. Long ago he formed an ideal conception of omnipotence and omniscience which he embodied in his gods. Whatever seemed unattainable to his desires (or forbidden to him) he attributed to these gods. One may say, therefore, that these gods were the ideals of his culture. Now he has himself approached very near to realizing this ideal, he has nearly become a god himself.

—SIGMUND FREUD

Distinctive Elements

- dogmatic restrictions
- archetypal symbols
- holier than thou (and thou knowest who thou art)

Key Adherents

- Catelyn Stark
- the High Sparrow
- Westerosi smallfolk

HAVE YOU EVER wished you had a deity to bless your conquest or justify a spontaneous beheading? Dealing with the ethics of commoners can be quite bothersome. The Faith of the Seven has the solution: get yourself a divine brand and spokesperson! In this precarious pre-winter economy, having a god on your side just makes sense. The Great Sept of Baelor is open for business. They have seven options to choose from, making it easier than ever to find just the right fit for you.

Whether your cause is exploitation, sexual repression, or just old-fashioned world domination, the clergy of King's Landing are ready to negotiate. They have agents that specialize in judgment, courage, and warfare. They have agents of fertility, purity, and wisdom. And if your business is a matter of life and death, they've got an agent for that, too. Make your way to the plaza at the top of Visenya's Hill. Stay awhile in their gardens and linger in the Hall of Lamps. They take pride in their hospitable, low-pressure environment. That is, unless they need to detain you on suspicion of sexual deviancy. In that case, your business becomes their business.

DEEP DIVE:
TOUGH LUCK, ROSIE COTTON

THE FAITH OF the Seven is Martin's most detailed religion. There's mythology, scripture, taboos, clerics, ceremonies, architecture, institutional power, reformers, armed forces, pacifist outliers, and poetry for children. The religion even comes with its own idioms and vulgarities. At the same time, it might be Martin's least magical invention.

If you want super-stealth assassins, go to Braavos. If you want a time-traveling spy network, go north. If you want blood magic, wait for an Asshai missionary to come knocking. The Faith of the Seven isn't for thrill seekers. The septons will facilitate your name day and marriage ceremony. They will oversee your trial by combat. The Silent Sisters will tend to your grandmother's corpse. And if you need a witness protection program, the local septry might help a brother out. But the Seven-Faced God isn't going to kill your enemies for you or beguile your enemies with a convincing glamour.

☙ Excursus: Forty and Five Fictional Facts about the Faith in Fun-Sized Font ❧

(1) The *Seven-Pointed Star* is the primary sacred text for the faith as passed down from the Andals. (2) The text claims that the seven gods of the Andals once walked among humans in the Hills of Andalos. (3) These seven form a union within one single deity. (4) This union is called "the Seven-Faced God" or more commonly "the Seven." (5) The Faith of the Seven is the most pervasive religion in Westeros. (6) Westerosi devotees pray to each of the Seven (or all of them) depending on the topic of their prayer. (7) The seven aspects of this god are the Father, Mother, Maiden, Crone, Warrior, Smith, and Stranger. (8) The Father functions as the judge of the living and dead. (9) The Mother governs fertility. (10) The Mother also represents mercy. (11) The Maiden is the goddess of purity and chastity. (12) In legend, the human patriarch of the Andals (Hugor of the Hill) took the Maiden as his bride. (13) The Crone is depicted as a wise, elderly woman carrying a lantern. (14) The Crone represents foresight. (15) The Warrior represents valor in warfare. (16) The Warrior is often prayed to for courage before and during battles. (17) The Smith represents creativity, specifically labor and craftsmanship. (18) The Andals were known for their craftsmanship of steel, particularly steel weaponry that allowed them to take much of Westeros from the "First Men." (19) Westerosi devotees pray to the Smith for help with broken things. (20) The Smith is depicted as a man holding an anvil. (21) The Stranger is without definitive gender. (22) The Stranger guides the deceased to the next world, thus representing death. (23) The Stranger is depicted variously as zoomorphic or as a human skeleton with flowing robes. (24) Places of worship are called septs and commonly are seven-walled structures. (25) Septs feature seven images representing the essential aspects of the Seven. (26) The Great Sept of Baelor is the largest place of worship within King's Landing and the seat of power for the religion in Westeros. (27) It was named for Baelor the Blessed, the Targaryen king who envisioned its creation. (28) The Great Sept is domed in marble and encircled by seven crystal towers. (29) Male clergy are called septons. (30) Chief among the faithful is the High Septon who resides in King's Landing. (31) Female clergy are called septas. (32) Female clergy who prepare bodies for burial are called Silent Sisters. (33) The Silent Sisters take a vow of silence. (34) Clergy to the faith are celibate, forsaking family names, titles, marriage, and progeny. (35) Clergy preside over major life transitions, including birth, marriage, and death. (36) A council of elite clergy called the "Most Devout" preside in King's Landing. (37) Before the Most Devout presided in King's Landing, they were located at the Starry Sept in Old Town. (38) The Most Devout includes both male and female clergy. (39) The Faith Militant is a military branch commanded by the High Septon. (40) Knights who join the Faith Militant are called "The Noble and Puissant Order of the Warrior's Sons," or more simply "Swords." (41) Commoners who join the Faith Militant are called the "Poor Fellows" or "Stars." (42) Adherents believe in seven heavens. (43) The Father welcomes repentant men and women to an eternal banqueting table after death. (44) Adherents believe in seven hells. (45) The "Lord of the Seven Hells" epitomizes evil and commands demonic forces.

47. J. R. R. Tolkien, *The Hobbit*, rev. ed. (New York: Random House, 1982), 4.

So why are the Seven so popular in Westeros? Why don't more people sign up for a religion with demonstrable power? Maybe—and bear with us—hobbits have the answer. "'We are plain quiet folk and have no use for adventures. Nasty disturbing uncomfortable things! Make you late for dinner! I can't think what anybody sees in them,' said our Mr. Baggins, and stuck one thumb behind his braces, and blew out another even bigger smoke-ring."[47]

Mind you, the smallfolk of Westeros are a bit more corruptible than hobbits. But in general, most people aren't interested in charging into battle (especially if victory requires a human sacrifice) or ascending to the Iron Throne (which usually means that you'll be miserable and short-lived). At the level of peasants, the Faith of the Seven is about tradition, continuity, predictability, structure, and comfort. Just substitute smoke-rings for incense and it's the perfect religion for hobbits.

As Ser Jorah reminds us, the smallfolk pray for good rain, healthy children, and long summers (*Game 23*, Daenerys III). These are the concerns of the average father and mother in Westeros. Westerosi fathers and mothers have developed ideals, hopes, and standards for themselves. They know what the ideal father and mother look like, what they care about, what they do. Such ideals are embodied in their gods: the Father and the Mother. These—the first two of the seven aspects of God—are necessary "archetypes" (idealized symbols) of fatherhood and motherhood.

Jorah's assessment reminds us how essential fertility is for agrarian cultures. The Mother (giver of life) and the Smith (the ideal laborer) uphold necessary standards for people who live and die with the harvest. The climate is just one factor in their well-being. Westerosi culture is deeply concerned with the probability of a long winter.

It looms large over every long-term hope. It makes sense that hard work is built into the national identity. Hard work before winter is critical to survival and has become spiritualized. There is perhaps nothing more primary to religion than a preoccupation with fertility and harvest.[48]

Hope for general health coupled with a sense of hard work result in a structured social psychology.[49] If you're a common laborer in Westeros, working in the fields or shoeing horses, it's virtuous to work hard. But it's more than that. When you're plowing, smithing, and cleaning stables you're becoming a better (more ideal) version of yourself. You're not just part of the structure of society; you're reinforcing the structure of your spiritual life. If you're a Westerosi maiden, society expects you to live up to an ideal of purity and eventually fall in love with some lucky smith. If you're a soldier, you are socially obligated to kill and/or die for your liege lord. If you're a woman, it's your job to produce more smiths, maidens, and soldiers for the realm. As Randall Tarly once bluntly stated, "The gods made men to fight, and women to bear children. A woman's war is in the birthing bed" (*Feast* 14, Brienne III).

This all might sound well and good if you're Lobelia Sackville-Baggins. But if you've got a bit of Took in you, you're probably suspicious about these types. After all, if society expects you to live up to an ideal, doesn't the archetype become a stereotype? And what if you're a woman who isn't interested in the Maiden-Mother-Crone cycle? Tough luck, Rosie Cotton, you're probably going to have to marry a fat gardener and have thirteen children. (The hobbit tradition of six meals per day might sound nice, but imagine cooking for fifteen Gamgees everyday.) Fertility is the lifeblood of agrarian life but it's also a yoke.

This brings us to the matter of enforcing the social structures. It also brings us—in a darker turn—from the

48. The use of the word "religion" here is probably anachronistic. But the myths and rituals related to fertility and harvest tend to evolve into social systems that modern minds associate with religion.

49. See C. G. Jung, *Collected Works of C. G. Jung,* vols. 1–20, ed. H. Read et al., trans. R. F. C. Hull et al. (New York: Princeton University Press, 1953–91), 3093–94. The notion of archetypes can be traced back to the Greek philosophy of ideal forms. But Jung put them to use in social psychology: "Archetypes are typical modes of apprehension, and wherever we meet with uniform and regularly recurring modes of apprehension we are dealing with an archetype, no matter whether its mythological character is recognized or not. The collective unconscious consists of the sum of the instincts and their correlates, the archetypes. Just as everybody possesses instincts, so he also possesses a stock of archetypal images."

peasants to the throne room. The Faith of the Seven is useful for fathers, lords, and kings because it gives them a divine obligation to judge and discipline.

One example is the "rule of six." This is the Westerosi law that a man can beat his wife with a stick no wider than his thumb and no more than six times.[50] The rule was handed down by Rhaenys Targaryen (sister and wife of Aegon). After learning that a man had beaten his wife to death for adultery, Queen Rhaenys consulted with maesters and septons to create a new rule. She granted that (1) the gods created women to be "dutiful" to their husbands and (2) husbands could, by law, beat their wives. But she decreed that no wife was to be struck more than six times, "one each for the Seven, save the Stranger, who was death" (*World*, Aegon I).

Clearly Westeros, as a general rule, places the value and desires of men above women. Look no further than the stories of Cersei, Sansa, and Jeyne for examples. What the story of Rhaenys adds is that the general rule of patriarchy is reinforced by theology. The faith teaches that husbands represent the will of the gods when beating their wives. Think of this like a mythological mirror whereby human fathers reflect the divine Father. Just as the Father judges and disciplines all of humanity, husbands are supposed to judge and discipline their wives. The husband, in a sense, is enacting the wrath of the gods. This is what passes for "progress" north of Dorne.

In the same way, the king enacts the will of the Seven as he rules over the Seven Kingdoms. This is the social structure of Westeros, divinely ordained. After Ned confesses his fabricated crimes, the High Septon declares, "As we sin, so do we suffer." He adds, "The gods are just, yet Blessed Baelor taught us that they are also merciful. What shall be done with this traitor, Your Grace?" (book

50. Here we have an echo to the English idiom "rule of thumb." While the history of this idiom is difficult to discern, it carries a folk (i.e., fake) etymology that English men in the 1800s were allowed to beat their wives provided that the stick was thinner than their thumb. The fact that this folktale is even plausible is troubling.

only; *Game* 65, Arya v).[51] In the end it is up to the king to judge. Luckily for the king, the Seven-Faced God is both a goddess of mercy and a god of discipline. Whatever Joffrey decrees, he's enacting divine will. *Translation: the Faith of the Seven allows those in power to act like gods and affords Joffrey the right to be a monster.*

Among fans, Joffrey has become a popular target for collective hatred. And for good reason: Joffrey is what would happen if Sid from Toy Story was sorted into House Slytherin while taking extracurricular karate at Cobra Kai. But usually lost in all of the justifiable Joffrey-hate is the complicity of the High Septon. It's his job, seemingly, to throw theological weight behind whatever whim comes into Joffrey's deranged mind.

For both the smallfolk and for those circling the Iron Throne, the worship of the Seven reinforces the existing power structures. To worship the Seven is to worship power.

Trial by combat illustrates this perfectly. In this tradition, the accused can call for a champion to defend him by combat. The gods demonstrate their will—judging the guilt or innocence of the accused—through the outcome of the fight. As usual, we agree with Tyrion, this tells us something about the gods (S04E08, "The Mountain and the Viper").

HISTORICAL BACKDROP: TWO FERTILITY DEITIES

FERTILITY GODS AND goddesses can be found in almost every ancient mythology. While Martin projects this aspect to the Mother, not every fertility myth involves women. For example, the following creation hymn was composed in the Old Kingdom of ancient Egypt.

51. In the HBO adaptation, these lines are given to Pycelle.

Deep Dive:
Tough Luck, Rosie Cotton

91

In this excerpt, we hear the voice of the Atum (or Tem), the first god, creator, and finisher:

Seven Hells!
Summa Septologica

> *When I first began to create*
> *When I alone was planning and*
> *designing many creatures,*
> *I had not sneezed Shu the wind,*
> *I had not spat Tefnut the rain,*
> *There was not a single living creature.*
>
> *. . .*
>
> *Then I copulated with my own fist.*
> *I masturbated with my own hand.*
> *I ejaculated into my own mouth.*
> *I sneezed to create Shu the wind,*
> *I spat to create Tefnut the rain.*
> *Old Man Nun reared them*
> *Eye the Overseer looked after them.*[52]

52. Translation from Victor H. Matthews and Don C. Benjamen, *Old Testament Parallels: Laws and Stories from the Ancient Near East*, 4th ed. (New York: Paulist, 2016), 8–9.

See, no women involved. Just a bit of general grossness with a healthy side of awkward yuck. But once you're over it—and do please give yourself a minute—it's kind of an awesome window into circa 2500 BCE. (Even better when sung to the tune of Bruno Mars' "Grenade.")

If you're not into this particular creation myth, there are lots of others. One interesting parallel to Martin's Maiden-Mother-Crone paradigm is from Hawaii. Haumea is the archetypal mother-goddess in Hawaiian mythology. Haumea gives birth to life using various body parts and sometimes takes human form. She variously appears as a crone and a young woman, symbolizing different stages of the female life cycle. Haumea also functions as a divine midwife that oversees childbirth. You can read more about her in the *Kumulipo*, an epic creation poem.

HISTORICAL BACKDROP:
WHY SEVEN?

THERE WERE FEW cultural forces in medieval Europe stronger or more pervasive than the Roman Catholic Church. It's symbols and mythos seeped into the pores of European life to create a new expression of Christianity. Martin attempts to capture the essence of this social force with the Faith of the Seven. In Westeros, this religion impacts the language, the interpretation of major events, how the maesters write history, and how king's rule. Even scoundrels and skeptics reinforce the legacy of the Andals when they curse or mock religion.[53] Martin explains that he drew from his own upbringing.

The Faith of the Seven is very loosely modeled on the medieval Catholic Church. But, of course, with different elements. . . . I'm no longer a practicing Catholic, but that was how I was born and raised. [The Catholic Church] has the whole concept of the Trinity, which was explained to be as: "it's three, but it's also one." Which kids can never get. It's like "okay, we have three gods."—"No, no, you don't have three gods, you have one God; he has three parts." . . . It was like the shamrock, you know, the three-leafed clover.[54]

In other words, as we learned in fancy-lad school, "One God in three persons: Father, Son, and Holy Spirit." Martin expands this from three to seven: Father,

Historical Backdrop: Two Fertility Deities

53. The tribe credited with bringing the Faith of the Seven to Westeros was called the "Andals." It's possible that this is an alliterative echo to the historical "Angles," a Germanic tribe that settled among the native Britons during (or soon after) the decline of the Roman Empire. It might also be an echo of Al-Andalus, which referred to Islamic Iberia (Spain).

54. Martin, "Talks at Google," YouTube, August 6, 2011.

Mother, Maiden, Crone, Warrior, Smith, and Stranger. But why seven?

Seven Hells!
Summa Septologica

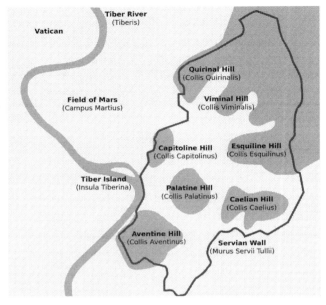

The Seven Hills of Rome: This topography shows the seven key hills of the city. In Latin, they are Aventinus, Cælius, Capitolinus, Esquilinus, Palatinus, Quirinalis, and Viminalis. Courtesy of Renata3 via Wikimedia Commons.

Seven is an interesting choice. It's a common biblical symbol, thought to symbolize completion or wholeness. But there might be another reason why there are seven aspects of God in Westeros, one that relates to ancient Rome. According to legend, the city of Rome was formed by uniting the tribes on the seven hills of Rome.

The city was so well known for this geography that it was known symbolically as "the Seven Hills."[55] The fact that there are seven gods in Westeros might be a nod to Roman history and legend. Hills, after all, are also the origin of the Faith of the Seven. The Andals, according

55. For example, see the book of Revelation 17:19.

94

to Westerosi mythology, once walked with their gods in the hills of Andalos. Their founding patriarch was named "Hugor of the Hill" (*World,* "The Arrival of the Andals"). Thus the mythical beginnings of both the Romans and the Andals involve hill-dwellers who expanded from their original geography.

Historical Backdrop:
Two Fertility Deities

Carrawburgh Mithraeum: This Mithraeum (temple to Mithras) near Brocolitia was used in the 3rd century by the Romans who defended Hadrian's Wall. Courtesy of Wikimedia Commons.

The pre-Christian Romans borrowed gods from Greek mythology, including the gods of the seven "classical planets": Sun, Moon, Mars, Mercury, Jupiter, Venus, and Saturn.[56] Continuing the theme of borrowing—in the same way the Borg "borrowed" technology in *Star Trek*—many Romans latched on to the cult of Mithras. Initiation into Mithraism involved seven key stages (and—no joke—a sacred handshake). Some Mithraic temples featured seven altars related to the following classifications: Raven, Bridegroom, Soldier, Lion, Persian (i.e.,

56. In this case, "planet" refers to the seven visible celestial bodies that seem to wander through the sky. We trace our seven days of the week to this sevenfold structure.

Perses), Courier of the Sun, and Father. At least two of these (Father and Soldier) are directly mirrored in the Westerosi Seven.

It is also likely that the Maiden mirrors the Roman Catholic veneration of the Virgin. Martin seems to have merged several aspects from several eras of Roman theology. Famously, the Roman Empire reached its northernmost point in England and was marked by Hadrian's Wall (inspiration for Martin's Wall).[57] In sum, the Andals expansion in Westeros parallels Rome's expansion into England.

57. The Mithraic temple at Carrawburgh is located along Hadrian's Wall.

CHARACTER STUDY: CATELYN

IN HER FIRST point-of-view chapter, Catelyn recalls the worship experience of her youth. She knew the seven faces of her god as well as she knew those of her parents. She felt comfortable in the sept at Riverrun. Worship included incense, rainbow-refracting crystals, and voices raised in song. Being a Tully meant being anointed with seven oils on your name day. It was a connection to her grandfather and his grandfather.

But her faith was also a reminder that she was not born in the North. Even though her husband had built her a sept at Winterfell, she would never share Ned's interior life with him. She felt alienated by the godswood where Ned would retire for prayer (*Game* 2, Catelyn I).[58] Catelyn embodies the difference and distance between the cultures of North and South. She is both the Lady of Winterfell and a displaced Tully from Riverrun. Unfortunately, this interesting aspect of Catelyn's duality is a book-only theme. Catelyn's prayer life, her outsider's perspective on Northern culture, and her feeling of being a fish out of water (pun intended) are muted in her HBO character.

58. Although later in her story she appears to pray to the old and new gods (*Clash* 45, 55, Catelyn VI, VII).

The portrayal of Catelyn by Benioff and Weiss (TVCat) is different from Martin's portrayal (BookCat) on several levels. First and foremost is that TVCat desperately wants Ned to stay in the North. She fears what might happen if he relocates to the South to assume his new office as Hand of the King. The showrunners completely reverse her primary motives. BookCat—who left her heart in the South—is almost pushing Ned out the door. It is his duty to serve at the king's pleasure and she pleads with Ned, despite his reluctance, to accept Robert's offer and become Hand of the King. In *Game,* Ned is determined to refuse Robert. But Catelyn pleads, "You cannot. You must not" (*Game* 6, Catelyn II).

Also, BookCat is not overly concerned with domestic stability. She's not even concerned with Ned's supposed infidelities (as long as she doesn't have to see his bastards). Catelyn is worried about maintaining good relations with King's Landing and with the possibility of conflict with the Baratheons. She's not driven by jealousy. BookCat has heard about the dead direwolf that was impaled by the antlers of a stag.[59] She takes this as an omen that points to conflict between the Baratheons and the Starks. BookCat cannot get the image of the omen out of her head. She's deeply worried that Ned might offend Robert and that the wrong step might lead to conflict. Call it religion or superstition, but BookCat sees the world in portents and symbols.

While TVCat has many of the same faults that Book-Cat has, TVCat might be more relatable. Actress Michelle Fairley somehow pulls off the magic trick of bringing expressive warmth to a character who is jealous of Ned's mistress, hates Jon Snow, and convinced of Tyrion's guilt. She's impetuous and not in Littlefinger's league in terms of political intrigue (very few are), but TVCat is ultimately

Character Study: Catelyn

59. Interestingly, this was the omen that foreshadowed the entire story for Martin. He claims to have begun with the image of a dead direwolf impaled by a stag's antlers. *A Song of Ice and Fire* grew around this initial scene. "Game of Throne's Creator Reveals Fantasy's Inspirations," ABC. net.au, video 6:24, posted November 11, 2013.

sympathetic. In one of her most revealing scenes, TVCat confesses her hatred for Jon Snow is wrapped with a sense of religious shame.

Building from her coldness to Jon Snow, TVCat recounts a story from when Jon was a child. Jon, she thought, was Ned's illegitimate son. She couldn't stand the sight of the boy; he was a reminder of her husband's infidelity. So Catelyn prayed to the gods for the boy to die.[60] Soon after, the boy became deathly ill. When she thought Jon might finally die one night, she had a change of heart. In her own words, "I knew I was the worst woman who ever lived" (S03E02, "Dark Wings, Dark Words"). She then prayed for the boy to live and wove a prayer wheel for him. She promised the Seven that if Jon Snow lived, she would love him and ask Ned to give him the name Stark. Of course, she couldn't keep her promise. Because of this—because she couldn't love a "motherless child"—TVCat blames herself for the ill fortune of the Stark family. This scene has no parallel in the books but it's wonderful story-telling in its own right. It brings out a level of self-aware-ness in Catelyn that also touches her darkly complicated relationship with the gods.

Although different, BookCat's self-awareness is no less dark: "I take no joy in mead nor meat, and song and laughter have become suspicious strangers to me." She continues, "I am a creature of grief and dust and bitter longings. There is an empty place within me where my heart was once" (*Clash* 55, Catelyn VII). After the collapse of House Stark, BookCat finds herself on a different path. No doubt this internal monologue foreshadows her trans-formation into Lady Stoneheart.[61]

Seven Hells!
Summa Septologica

60. According to Dr. Le Donne, "This is what we call in the seminary biz a 'dick move.'"

61. Incidentally, A.Ron and Anthony differ on which Catelyn is more compelling. Anthony prefers BookCat: "The way I read BookCat is as a character with deep duality. She's both Lady of Winterfell and a daughter of Riverrun. Eventually her fondness for her southron roots wins out and is her undoing." A.Ron prefers TVCat: "TVCat has a lot more humanity than BookCat. And that's BookCat before she gets transformed into an undying rage zombie. BookCat has the same plot foibles as TVCat, such as impetuously arresting Tyrion, freeing Jaime, and loathing Jon Snow. The show just gives her the grace to be self-aware enough of that latter fact to be self-loathing. It's just hard for me to hate a person who judges themselves as harshly as I ever could."

CHARACTER STUDY:
THE HIGH SPARROW

ONE OF THE most powerful players in King's Landing is the so-called High Sparrow. After Tywin has been murdered and Cersei has been imprisoned, the new High Septon holds the best cards in the capital. Moreover, his sway with Tommen gives him a level of privilege and security that only Margery can rival.

The High Sparrow is devoted to purity, not interested in alliances, and refuses to bend his agenda for political expediency. In some ways, he is very much like Ned Stark in character. He is strong-willed and deeply committed to his system of ethics. According to Cersei, he is "implacable" (*Dance* 54, Cersei 1). But so far he has managed to avoid beheading.[62]

62. This is one of those times when we remain unconvinced by the HBO depiction of a character's outcome. We don't doubt that the High Sparrow will come to some horrific and unnatural end. But we doubt that Martin's narrative will burn half of the elite of King's Landing in the Great Sept. This event seems like the showrunners' way to narrow the plot due to their time constraints.

☙ Excursus: Ascetic Spirituality ❧

Ascetic spirituality became a popular form of religious observance in medieval Christianity. In this case, "ascetic" means severe self-control and discipline that leads to a more devoted spiritual state. Of course, Christianity didn't invent the idea. Various philosophers and athletes (especially among the Greeks) promoted physical discipline and abstinence from comfort to achieve a larger goal. In extreme forms, self-flagellation and other forms of self-harm became avenues for spiritual devotion. But more commonly ascetics refrained from marriage, progeny, and a variety of foods and

> drink. For example, Benedictine and Franciscan monasteries trace their vows of poverty, humility, celibacy, etc., to Benedict (ca. 480–547) and Francis (ca. 1182–1226). Both groups maintain a long and detailed list of rules for monastic life.[63]

63. See, for example, "The Rule of Benedict," the Order of Saint Benedict, www.osb.org/rb/.

His pre-septon name is unknown (which is common among Faith of the Seven clerics) and we know very little of his backstory. But he is reminiscent of several Christian mystics in the medieval period. Characteristics like his vow of poverty and his rise in popularity echo saints like Benedict of Nursia and Francis of Assisi. Like these examples, the High Sparrow continues his vow of poverty even after his followers have elevated him in rank. In stark contrast to the previous High Septon, he continues to wear a simple wool tunic. Rather than wearing the traditional golden headpiece, he sells it and uses the money for the poor. He is thin, austere, and (seemingly) without vanity.

He's also similar to many religious ascetics who punish themselves physically as an act of spiritual devotion. The High Sparrow claims to feel closer to the Seven when he's being whipped (*Feast* 44, Cersei x). But the parallels with monastic ascetics can only be taken so far, because none of these examples become papal demagogues.

After his rise to popularity, his militant "sparrows" crash a meeting of the Most Devout (akin to a papal conclave). The meeting was meant to replace the recently killed High Septon with another wealthy, elite member of their own group. Intimidated by the uprising, the committee selects the nameless, unshod ascetic (*Feast* 28, Cersei vi). This is how the ever-humble sparrow rises to power.

Clearly Martin has been inspired by the Protestant Reformation in a few ways. George confesses, "The Sparrows are my version of the medieval Catholic Church." He explains that church history includes "periods where you had very worldly and corrupt popes and bishops. People who were not spiritual, but were politicians." Martin depicts this with the High Septon who serves during Robert's reign. This guy was openly regarded as corrupt and self-serving (with a physique round enough to make Robert Baratheon jealous). Eventually he is torn to pieces by a starving mob—perhaps contributing to a few "bowls of brown" in Flea Bottom. The new High Septon, according to Martin, is very different.

Character Study:
The High Sparrow

> *But you also had periods of religious revival or reform—the greatest of them being the Protestant Reformation, which led to the splitting of the church—where there were two or three rival popes each denouncing the other as legitimate. That's what you're seeing here in Westeros. The two previous High Septons we've seen, the first was very corrupt in his own way, and he was torn apart by the mob during the food riots. The one Tyrion appoints in his stead is less corrupt but is ineffectual and doesn't make any waves. Cersei distrusts him because Tyrion appointed him. So now she has to deal with a militant and aggressive Protestant Reformation, if you will, that's determined to resurrect a faith that was destroyed centuries ago by the Targaryens.[64]*

64. James Hibberd, "'Game of Thrones': George R. R. Martin Reveals Which Religion Inspired the Faith Militant," *ew.com*, May 24, 2015

Historically speaking, Martin Luther doesn't become a rival pope. Nor was Luther a thin man. The sparrows carry their leader into the center of power on their shoulders. This never happened with Luther. We doubt if all the cardinals in Germany could have lifted Martin Luther off the ground.[65]

Luther does, however, rail against the exploitative practices of an excessively wealthy church. This is an obvious parallel to the agenda of the High Sparrow. Also, Luther was notorious for his iron will. But really, we could say the same of most ascetic, social reformers. So Martin's passing mention of the Reformation should be taken with a grain of salt. The High Sparrow doesn't seem to parallel any key personality during the Reformation. The crucial difference is that the High Sparrow uses his platform to resurrect a crusadesque military branch: the Faith Militant.

His ability to convince Cersei to legalize his military agenda coupled with his influence over (recently crowned) Tommen make the High Sparrow dangerous. It is possible that he's simply a true believer who wants to enforce sexual restrictions and regular prayer. It is also possible that he is playing his own version of the game of thrones with the help of some other (silent) partner(s). The fact that we know so little about his backstory makes us suspicious. *Is there anyone in Martin's world that isn't driven by family honor, self-interest, or a desire for more power?*

One thing is certain: political forces that build militaries tend to use them.

65. Lest you think we're being hard on Luther, neither of your humble, cuddly authors have missed many meals. And Luther himself was pretty self-deprecating. A few days before his death, he was reported to joke with his friends that he would "give the worms a fat doctor to feast on" (Lyndal Roper, "Martin Luther's Body: The 'Stout Doctor' and His Biographers," *American Historical Review* 115.2 [2010]: 351–84).

FAN THEORY FUN:
MAESTER MACHINATIONS

AFTER THE WHOLE Mt. Doom episode with Frodo, Sam hops narratives and lands in Oldtown. There he learns from Marwyn that the maesters are not the neutral scholars and medics they appear to be. Rather, the establishment at the Citadel has been moving political chess pieces around for centuries. The maesters (at least the elite among them) have been conspiring to rid the world of magic, especially dragon magic. Or, at least, this is what Marwyn tells him. "Who do you think killed all the dragons the last time around?" Marwyn answers his own question, "The world the Citadel is building has no place in it for sorcery or prophecy or glass candles, much less for dragons" (*Feast* 78, Samwell v). The jury is out, however, on whether Marwyn is a reliable historian, misinformed, or just nuts. There's no doubt that he's accomplished, well-traveled, and talented. But his reputation at the Citadel is dubious.

If correct, the usual story about the dragons dying off because of captivity is propaganda. In Marwyn's version of events, the maesters somehow drove the Targaryen beasts to extinction. They theorized that killing off the dragons would significantly diminish the efficacy of magic (of all kinds) in Westeros.[66] In short, the powerbrokers of the Citadel are trying to build a world without necromancers, maegi, weirwood, etc. Foremost on this agenda is the removal of Targaryens—hence dragons—from power.[67]

Taking this conspiracy a step further, some fans have argued that the maesters are the true powerbrokers behind the Faith of the Seven. In secret, while preserving a veneer of neutrality, the Citadel has promoted (maybe even invented) the Seven-Faced God. *Why would scholars*

66. It is commonly assumed that dragon magic is the source of many of other kinds of magic. It's hard to say whether the link is casual, causal, or coincidental, but practitioners as diverse as the warlocks of Pree and the pyromancers of King's Landing agree that their powers have increased since Dany's miracle babies. We will address this topic more fully in volume 2.

67. This is often referred to as the "Grand Maester Conspiracy" and it's got several working parts, including Marwyn's nefarious students, the Faceless Men, and alternative history of Robert's Rebellion. See the early musings of Fire Eater, "The Citadel's Grand Conspiracy," A Forum of Ice and Fire (fan forum), posted November 24, 2011.

devoted to science and history do such a thing? Answer: in their effort to replace magic, they constructed a civic religion—one without supernatural power with pliable and flexible teachings, making it easier to control. The Seven-Faced God allows the smallfolk to cling to something heartening in a heartless land.[68] The faith functions (to paraphrase Marx) as milk of the poppy for the populace.

For our part, we doubt that such a plot will surface in the HBO version. The showrunners simply don't have enough screen time to develop it and Sam (show only) has already left the Citadel behind. If the maester conspiracy does surface, it will probably be a book-only plot.

BIRD'S-EYE VIEW: BEYOND TOLKIEN'S SHADOW

IT IS IMPOSSIBLE to measure the impact that Tolkien's imagination had on Martin. But it's safe to say that the impact was considerable. Tolkien's genius made a Manderly-sized cannonball splash into the fantasy genre.[69] So in addition to several direct literary allusions to the original R. R., Martin's pirate ship (even when he is truly original) floats atop Tolkien's oceanic crest. This is true when Martin plays with high fantasy tropes and it is especially true when Martin subverts them.

That said, Martin's treatment of ancient and medieval religion (especially religious pluralism) is unique. No doubt other fantasy authors play with religious themes and invent religious backdrops, but not quite like George. In this way—and we do not say this without great fear and trembling—Martin's imagination outshines Tolkien's shadow.

Tolkien (the devout Catholic) dug deep with mythology and language. And there's no doubt that certain biblical types bleed into *Lord of the Rings*. But where are the churches, monasteries, and temples in Middle Earth? The hobbits have seen Gandalf perform magic for decades; why isn't there a shrine venerating him in the Shire? Better yet, Eru is clearly the Divine Creator of Arda. Where is Thingol's ritual devotion? Why doesn't Fëanor develop the Valinor Tree cult that opposes the eagle religion of Manwë? The answer to all of these questions, of course, is that Tolkien wasn't giving us a religious sociology. This simply wasn't his intention. As irony would have it, it took a proudly lapsed Catholic to give us a fantasy landscape with robust, textured, and compelling religious pluralism.

A large part of Martin's interest in Christianity relates to his aim to exploit the social conditions of the War of the Roses. The Faith of the Seven certainly grows from this soil. We'd be selling Martin short, however, if we dismissed this religion as a simple mirror image of Christianity. He could have simply infused the history with a single religion as Geoffrey of Monmouth did with Arthurian legend. Instead we find aspects of many religions (ancient, medieval, and modern) in Westeros. And we see the virtues and vices of Christianity in several competing religions in Martin's world.

Perhaps Tolkien was too entrenched in his own religion to see it with the benefit of hindsight. Or perhaps Tolkien was too solemn about his own religion to play with it as a literary toy. Whatever the case, we are grateful that he didn't try. Middle Earth, as fantasy landscapes goes, is something close to perfect. A random temple to Ilúvatar might have ruined it. Conversely, we cannot image the *Ice and Fire* landscape without religious pluralism. It brings a level of realism to Martin's world that transcends Tolkien's genre. It is highly likely that Martin's setting would feel derivative without it.

Bird's-Eye View:
Beyond Tolkien's Shadow

The Faithless and the Hound
A CHAPTER ABOUT OUR FAVORITE SKEPTICS

5

If lightning is the anger of the gods, then the gods are concerned mostly about trees.

—LAO TZU

Distinctive Elements
- devotion to the tangible
- moral flexibility
- professional drunkenness
- eating every chicken in the room

Key Adherents
- Tyrion Lannister
- Cersei Lannister
- Qyburn
- Sandor Clegane

TRAVEL GUIDE

NEED TO GET away? Whether you're escaping the wrath of your bloodthirsty sister, or just need a holiday, consider sailing to beautiful Pentos! This ancient city is home to the music-loving and avant-garde Pentoshi. Their wine is exquisite, and their cheeses are even better. Visit the walled gardens of Illyrio. These gardens are a favorite destination for highborn refugees and a lovely locale for suicidal ideation.

*The Faithless and the
Hound: A Chapter about
Our Favorite Skeptics*

THE BIZARRE DYSFUNCTIONS of the Lannister family are a morality dumpster fire. But on a cold night, the heat is almost worth the stink. The Lannisters are rotten with deceit, conceit, emotional abuse, addiction, incest, and attempted murder—and sometimes they *really* get nasty. In Tyrion's first point-of-view chapter, we witness firsthand the fascinating dynamics of Tywin's irreligious progeny (*Game* 9, Tyrion 1). The use of religious language by Cersei and Tyrion is telling.

Tyrion is arguably Martin's most complex and empathetic character. He's sardonic, self-aware, clever, and wounded to his core. Tyrion's story begins with an exchange between the self-described dwarf bastard[70] and his soon-to-be-king nephew. After Joffrey refuses to console the grieving Starks, Tyrion slaps the smug right off his Justin Bieber face. Martin somehow bewitches us into loving Tyrion for this. We've certainly never met a single reader who is offended by Joffrey-slapping, and we know the entire internet.[71] After slapping the boy a second time, Tyrion instructs him to go to the grieving Starks and offer his thoughts and prayers. But, of course, this assumes that Joffrey has prayed, he is going to pray, or he is going to lie about praying.

In truth, Joffrey hasn't been praying for the Starks and he has no intention of doing so. An argument could be made that neither thinks prayer would do them any good. But even if Joffrey hasn't prayed and Tyrion is a skeptic of prayer, this is the sort of thing that must be said by a Baratheon prince to a Stark lord. Put another way, Tyrion is attempting to slap some political sense into him. Tyrion

70. We will use the term "dwarf," which is internal to the narrative and at home in medical terminology. We realize that this term may not be preferred as a self-referent in the modern world. There is also reason to think (discussed below) that Martin is playing with a fantasy trope. Also, because this is a book about gods, we would be remiss if we didn't also mention that Tyrion proclaims himself the "God of Tits and Wine" (S03E08, "Second Sons").

71. Child abuse is wrong. But Joffrey is the proud owner of a *Backpfeifengesicht*, which of course is the German word for a face that cries out to be slapped. You have to admire precision German verbal engineering.

knows that playing the political game often requires a veneer of religious language.

After his morning Joffrey-slap session, Tyrion joins the company of Jaime and Cersei. The twins are eating breakfast and eager to hear news of Bran Stark's medical condition. Jaime and Cersei are well aware that Bran has "accidentally" fallen from a tower. Bran might survive, albeit crippled. This surprises the dirty duo and Cersei complains that northern gods must be cruel. *Does she believe in the northern gods?* Tyrion, when asked if Bran will wake, concedes that only the gods know. *Does he believe that gods take interest in such matters?*

Deep Dive: Lannister Theology

It's possible that Tywin's kids believe in the gods on some level. (For example, Cersei isn't skeptical enough to disregard a woods-witch prophecy and worries at times about the wrath of the gods; *Storm* 62, Jaime VII.) But the god-talk of Cersei and Tyrion rarely reveals their true theology. They are, rather, fluent in the language of politics. So when they want to communicate without revealing too much, god-talk will be baked into the cowchip cookies. The Lannisters have learned this after years of networking King's Landing, seat of the High Septon.

The *realpolitik* of Westeros demands winks and nods to pious folk and religious zealots, whether you're a believer or not. Conversely, those who fail to play the religious game well usually fail at politics, too. If we follow Cersei's arc, we see that she hits rock-bottom when she fails to appreciate the political power of the High Sparrow (*Feast* 36, 43, Cersei VIII, X). Giving new meaning to the "walk of shame," Cersei is bested by a religious reformer who outmaneuvers her (S05E10, "Mother's Mercy").

Tyrion hits his lowest point differently but continues to theologize as he descends. Tyrion is accused of killing his nephew, the late king. He demands trial by combat to let the gods decide his fate (presumably, the gods favor the champion of the innocent). When Tyrion's champion is defeated, his reputation as a kinslayer is set in stone. The gods, in essence, have judged him to be both kingslayer and kinslayer. Tyrion will carry this curse—*like Cain from Genesis*—for the rest of his life. He, by way of jailbreak, is then freed to walk the earth—*like Caine from Kung Fu*—from town to town, meet people, get into adventures.

His first adventure is a visit to the Tower of the Hand. Tyrion has already been convicted of kinslaying, which is cursed by gods and men (*Clash* 44, Tyrion X; *Dance* 27, Tyrion VII). He has also been accused by his sister of killing his mother, who died giving birth to him. Tyrion decides, therefore, to live up to his reputation.

HISTORICAL BACKDROP: ANCIENT PHYSIOGNOMY

ANCIENT GREEK AND Roman leaders were often judged by appearance. Of course, this is still true in modern societies, but the authors of physiognomic literature developed a (pseudo)science that judged a man's character by measuring physical indicators. Zoomorphic comparison was foundational for judging men's personalities (and yes, it was almost always men). Lions, for example, were thought to be both courageous and generous. So to praise a leader's virtues was literally to lionize him. In this literature, eyes are most important. Overly large eyes indicated a bovine character and such men were thought to be docile. *Who wants to follow a cow?* Having small or shifty eyes like a rodent was less than ideal. *A man with the moral character of a rat is not to be trusted!*

Extremes in physical appearance were also important indicators. If a man's skin was too pale or too dark, he was less than ideal. Overly curly or straight hair would be a problem (Caligula was rumored to be pale of skin with dark, straight hair; he would practice grimacing in the mirror in his free time). Stature was also important for physiognomy. Being too tall or too short was less than ideal. Moderation in all things was preferable. (See, for example, Pseudo-Aristotle's *Physiognomonica* and Polemo's *De Physiognomonia*.)

While on trial for murder, Tyrion claims that he is only guilty of being a dwarf. More to the point, he has been on trial for his dwarfism his whole life (S04E06, "The Laws of Gods and Men"). This statement rings true, especially if Tyrion lives in a world that judges his character by physiognomy. His stature notwithstanding, Tyrion's mismatched eyes (one green; one black) would have been especially suspicious to the medieval mind. A man like Tyrion would be an easy target for blame, simply because his appearance would suggest something sinister in his soul.[72]

Regardless of whether Tyrion is really cursed, he starts to act like it. He descends into suicidal depression, fixating on the worst moments of his life. Tyrion escapes across the Narrow Sea—*like Jonah from Jonah*—and wonders if the storm is a punishment from the "Father Above" for his kinslaying.[73] While in Illyrio's garden, Tyrion fixates on seven poisonous mushrooms. He pockets them, knowing that they will be lethal if eaten. The number seven is significant to him. He thinks the Seven (the gods of his birth religion) might be inviting him to end his life (*Dance* 1, Tyrion 1).[74]

This is Tyrion at his most vulnerable and exposed. When we first meet him he uses a veneer of religious language to cover his skepticism. But his skepticism isn't thoroughgoing. At his core, Tyrion has a complicated theology. He cannot be called an atheist in the modern

72. Ancient Egypt, however, revered dwarves and believed in at least two deities portrayed with dwarfism. Ker Than, "Ancient Egyptians Held Dwarves in High Esteem," *Live Science*, December 28, 2005, livescience.com. Of course, such reverence did not ensure that Egyptian little people were always humanized in Egyptian society. As is often the case with disability, the social stigma renders one either more or less than human.

73. There are a number of Jonah parallels here. The most striking are that Tyrion and Jonah are both suicidal (compare Jonah 1:12; 4:3; 4:9), they both travel by boat, below deck (Jonah 1:5), and they both attribute a storm to divine retribution (Jonah 1:12). There are also several important differences between Tyrion and Jonah. While these parallels may suggest literary echoes, we see no evidence of allegory.

74. A note on Pentoshi religion: Pentos is ruled by a council of magisters. But they appoint a figurehead to "rule" from among the elite families of the city. This prince is responsible for Pentoshi affairs on both land and sea (he enacts this ritually by sex with a land maiden and a sea maiden annually). If a lost war or famine befalls the city, the prince is ritually sacrificed to appease the gods. For more on similar ancient rituals in the ancient world, see René Girard, *Violence and the Sacred*, trans. Patrick Gregory (Baltimore: Johns Hopkins University Press, 1977). Girard explores the blurred lines between royalty and human sacrifice.

sense. He is more like Diagoras of Melos (5th c.) who mocks the gods and is banished from Athens. Diagoras is called an "atheist," meaning, in this context, that he is "godless." (For atheism in a more modern sense, see the speech by Salladhor Saan; S02E02, "The Night Lands").

Tyrion is godless in at least two ways: (1) his constantly irreverent humor; (2) the gods are against him. According to Martin, Tyrion's unfortunately twisted body is proof that he is "hated by the gods."[75] Although Tyrion's rational mind knows better, he has internalized a medieval understanding of godlessness.

Turning our attention back to Cersei, we have a less-subtle example of godlessness. Burning down the Great Sept of Baelor and every pious person in the city is a hint (show only). She's not a fan of organized religion. More importantly, Cersei rejects several Westerosi traditions. She shows little regard for the taboos of kingslaying, kinslaying, incest, no wine before noon, etc. She even cheats on her brother with her younger cousin.

Cersei's support and employment of Qyburn fits hand-in-glove with a medieval sense of godlessness. Qyburn is something of a Frankenstein/Galileo figure in Martin's world. He has been ostracized by the establishment and stripped of maester status. While the maesters are not a religious organization, they work within the social order of the realm. As such, the Citadel's sense of propriety leaves little room for Qyburn's dark curiosity.

Almost every culture that values ritual purity is deeply concerned with the elements of life and death. Whether the culture bans shellfish or shames smoking, to be "pure" is to work in harmony with the natural cycles of life and death. In medieval Europe, dissecting the deceased clashed with these sensibilities. It was tantamount to tampering in God's business.

The Faithless and the Hound: A Chapter about Our Favorite Skeptics

75. "The Real History behind Game of Thrones: Part One," YouTube video, 18:13, published November 16, 2017; this quotation by Martin will be explored more fully below.

If a man like Qyburn had lived in premodern Chris-
tendom, he would have easily achieved heretic status.
Worse, he would have been accused of being in league
with the devil. Attempting to animate a corpse with magic
could get you exiled or executed. In Martin's world, the
consequences Qyburn's "defrocking" is far less severe. He's
shunned by the maesters, but he's free to rise through
the Lannister ranks without much difficulty. Indeed, his
facility with "horrors" is intriguing to Cersei (*Dance*
54, Cersei 1).

Historical Backdrop:
Ancient Physiognomy

Qyburn's central role in the story is as Cersei's
resident mad scientist. He reanimates the dead corpse
of Gregor Clegane and renames him Ser Robert Strong.
Qyburn and his monster become Cersei's secret weapons.
Both seem to obey her every command and are chiefly
occupied with her defense.

While there is no doubt that Ser Robert Strong is
a type of Frankenstein's monster, there are other literary
analogies worth considering. One possible comparison
is Osiris, of Egyptian mythology. Osiris is torn limb from
limb and then stitched back together. He returns from
the dead to teach his son Horus how to best avenge him.
But perhaps the best analogy for Ser Robert Strong is the
golem myth from Jewish lore.

❧ *Excursus: The Golem* ❧

Premodern Jewish mythology tells of a subhu-
man creation called the golem. In most iterations of the story, the golem is formed of clay or
mud and then animated by a rabbi or sage. In early
forms of the myth, the golem is unable to speak,
lacking human intelligence. But the golem is usually

obedient, following directions well (albeit taking some directions too literally). As the myth evolves in later centuries, the golem gets too large to control or goes on a violent rampage.

The golem is created by writing the holy name of God (or a variation of it) on the creature's forehead or inserting a piece of paper with the name into its mouth. In some stories, the word for "truth" is used. In order to decommission the golem, one letter is removed, changing the word from "truth" to "dead." The most famous golem myth is set in 16th-century Prague. In this story, the golem is created to protect Jews against anti-Semitic attacks.

First, both Frankenstein's monster and Osiris are intelligent and able to speak. But like the golem, Ser Robert is mute and functions as an automaton. Second, neither Frankenstein's monster nor Osiris serve as a personal bodyguard. But like the golem, Ser Robert's primary purpose is to defend. Indeed he is reanimated specifically to fight Cersei's enemies.

Ser Robert's story and golem mythology differ, however, in their religious significance. The golem is created by a holy man to defend the pious. By contrast, Ser Robert is reanimated by an infidel and thought to be an abomination. So it seems that Ser Robert Strong is stitched together using parts of multiple fictions.

CHARACTER STUDY: JAIME

JAIME LANNISTER IS almost the perfect puzzle. Is he a moral monster? Is he an admirable member of the Kingsguard? Is he a good brother and son? Does he honor his ancestors and produce Lannister progeny for the well-being of his house? Put simply: *Is Jaime a good guy?*

It's a question that Martin refuses to answer in any neat way within the narrative. Jaime, no doubt, is introduced as a villain (just ask Bran Stark). But at times he slips easily into the role of the knight in shining armor, leading some fans to profess their Jaime-love without reservation. These fans love him from his Nuke Laloosh head to his Inigo Montoya fencing stance. But most of us feel a bit guilty about our Jaime crushes. Especially since the showrunners serve up an even darker portrait (cousin-killer and rapist).

For readers who want a bit of company in their golden-boy affection, we'd like to point you to Friedrich Nietzsche. We appeal to Doktor Mustache for one simple reason: Nietzsche, we believe, would think very highly of Jaime Lannister. Indeed, Nietzsche wouldn't just *like* Jaime; he would say that Jaime is heroically good, a paragon of virtue.

Nietzsche's moral ideal is a "higher type" of human being (Übermensch is translated variously as *overman, superman, beyond-man, higher type*).[76] This person displays five key attributes: he is "*solitary, pursues a 'unifying project,' is healthy, is life-affirming, and practices self-reverence.*"[77] Let's take each attribute in turn.

(1) Solitary. Here Nietzsche means that the higher type is self-reliant, avoiding the herd. The higher type is constantly contradicting the masses in both word and deed. He only relates to others as tools, obstacles in his way, or as temporary places to rest.

Jaime passes the first test with flying colors. He is solitary. He clearly believes that he is unique in the world. He exploits the affection of Alton Lannister and kills him without a second thought (show only; S02E07, "A Man Without Honor"). And while it takes thousands of pages to get there, he eventually sheds Cersei's affection. But

76. This section will use the generic gendered forms of "man," "he," and "him" to reflect Doktor Mustache's (less than progressive) tendencies.

77. Brian Leiter, "Nietzsche's Moral and Political Philosophy," *Stanford Encyclopedia of Philosophy* (online), first published August 26, 2004, revised October 7, 2015.

the case in point for Jaime's singularity is his slaying of the Mad King. He chooses his own path and lives up to his own standards without feeling the need to justify his actions to the rest of the kingdom. A lion does not concern itself with the opinions of sheep.

(2) A unifying project. Nietzsche is enamored with great, artistic types (e.g., Beethoven, Goethe). He loves men who pursue creative genius with a vengeance. The higher type is usually a guy who burns hot and bright—perhaps burning out quickly—and leaves behind a masterpiece.

Jaime's devotion to swordplay fits well here. Jaime regards swordplay as a high art and considers himself the great artist of his generation. He also has laser-beam focus on his career in the Kingsguard. Everything else is secondary.

(3) Healthy. By "healthy," Nietzsche means resilient. The higher type of human is instinctually committed to self-preservation and vitality. Even sickness is an opportunity for becoming more resilient.

Jaime's general health is important but his resilience is key. Although he navel gazes a bit after his encounter with Vargo/Locke (we imagine lots of philosophizing about one-handed clapping), he overcomes his loss. It is the will to overcome that interests Nietzsche.

(4) Life-affirming. In affirming his own life, the higher type affirms every part of himself. He is willing to relive his past again and again for eternity. The higher type would even relive his worst moments of suffering and not ask for an alternative path if given the choice. He has embraced every part of his past and present. Nietzsche uses himself as an example when he says he is in love with his own fate.

His brief identity crisis notwithstanding, Jaime refuses to live his life with regret. We get the sense that he would do it all over again: his long affair with Cersei, his youthful devotion to the divine "Warrior," his slaying of the Mad King, his time in prison, his adventure with Brienne. Even when reflecting on the arrogance of his youth, he continues to boast of his talent (*Storm* 67, Jaime VIII).

(5) Self-reverence. Nietzsche claims that the higher type has an ultimate faith in himself (this being the highest form of faith). To be noble, according to Nietzsche, is to be certain of your own nobility. The higher type reveres himself as a lesser man would revere a god.

On this point, Jaime's exchange with Catelyn reveals his self-reverential faith. When being interrogated by Lady Stark, he openly doubts the existence of any gods. What good did the tree gods do for Ned Stark? If there are gods, why is the world rife with pain and injustice? Lady Stark answers that the world is full of pain and injustice because of evil men. Men like Jaime Lannister. Jaime replies, "There are no men like me. There's only me" (*Clash* 55, Catelyn VII). Clearly, Jaime's faith in himself is more certain than in any notion of divinity.

So you would get a decisive answer if you asked Nietzsche, *Is Jaime a good guy?* Nietzsche would say, *Ja! He's a super-good guy!* It's also possible that Nietzsche wouldn't be all that grossed out by the rumors of Jaime's incest. After all, a rumor or two surfaced about Nietzsche and his own sister. Even if untrue, the higher type doesn't concern himself with the morality of the masses.

Dr. Mustache does have one serious flaw with his criteria. His five attributes give us reason to praise the virtues of someone like Beethoven (and Daenerys

78. Our thanks to Dr. Chad T. Carmichael on this point. Chad calls this counterexample the "Darth Vader Problem." His basic point is that if Nietzsche's "virtues" can be legitimately applied to a clearly antagonistic agent, this creates a problem for Nietzsche.

79. Friedrich Nietzsche, *Beyond Good and Evil* (London: Penguin, 1973), 118.

Targaryen for that matter). But wouldn't the same five attributes apply to Hannibal Lecter and Emperor Palpatine?[78]

It is also worth pointing out that Nietzsche would frown on Jaime's respect and affection for Brienne.[79] In his view, Brienne represents only a "delay" in Jaime's life. At this point, we must part ways with Nietzsche, no matter how much we admire his magnificent mustache. We don't see Jaime's acts of altruism as chinks in his armor. On the contrary, Brienne brings out the very best in him. Jaime Lannister may not be a *good guy* but he is capable of goodness nonetheless.

CHARACTER STUDY: SANSA

WHEN SANSA STARK is first introduced, she is little more than a two-dimensional character. Martin will eventually transform her into one of his more interesting actors. But at first glance, Sansa exists only to show us what Arya isn't. Arya is boyish, troublesome, restless, and lacking in the grace expected of noble ladies at court. To emphasize Arya's idiosyncrasies, Martin sits her next to Sansa by way of contrast. The older sister is also aloof and superficial, giving the reader an initial reason to empathize with the younger.

In her journey to King's Landing, Sansa is hopelessly—most fans would add, *wretchedly*—naïve. You could even make the case that her willful ignorance makes her worse than naïve; she's morally negligent. Her decision to lie in order to protect Joffrey (instead of Arya) results in the death of her direwolf. Not only does Sansa lose her pet, she loses the embodiment of her house sigil. This is Martin's way of suggesting a loss of identity. Again and again, Sansa plays the part of a pawn, allowing herself to be used by the Cerseis and Petyrs of the world. In Martin's world, to be spineless is to be amoral.

Crathes Castle Garden: Crathes Castle (Scotland) boasts nearly four acres of walled garden. It is not uncommon for castle grounds to have some form of a walled garden including mature trees like the one pictured here. In earlier periods, there was a strong link between gardens and temples. Many early temples were built to mirror sacred garden space. Photograph by Ikiwaner; courtesy of Wikimedia Commons.

It is no accident, then, that Sansa repeatedly visits the King's Landing godswood for prayer. The fact that this is a fake weirwood grove is important. There are no true weirwood trees in the capital. Rather, the grove is of elm, alder, and black cottonwood. Eventually she ceases praying altogether, and goes to the grove simply to be alone. Her religious life mirrors her professed love for Joffrey. Both are clumsily designed deceptions. The same could be said of her sham marriage to Tyrion.

Petyr Baelish (überperv) rightly informs her that every person in the capital is a liar. Moreover, everyone there is a better liar than Sansa. But as her story unfolds, she learns to play the political game better than her father ever did; she becomes a better and more strategic liar.

Sansa's facility with deception directly corresponds with her divorce from the religion of her youth.

Sansa's guise as "Alayne Stone" while at the Eyrie continues to play on the loss-of-identity theme.[80] The godswood at the Eyrie is little more than a garden. Instead of a Heart Tree, it features a statue of a weeping woman (*Feast* 41, Alayne 11). Sansa continues her tutelage in intrigue under Baelish but is still one of his pawns.

Indeed, Sansa will not truly find herself until she returns to Winterfell as Lady of the House. While under the Winterfell Heart Tree with Bran, she attempts to pass the lordship to him. When Bran refuses in the creepiest way possible, Sansa knows the care of Winterfell is in her hands. This is the same place—under the Winterfell Heart Tree—that Sansa finally rejects Baelish's advances (show only; S06E10, "The Winds of Winter"). She is done with praying but she is also done running from her life in the North.

CHARACTER STUDY: THE HOUND

"**I** GUESS I HAVE always been partial to rogues." So says Martin.[81] We agree, and Sandor "the Hound" Clegane is no exception. The Hound is a cauldron of the Sundance Kid, Han Solo, Jules Winnfield, and Anton Chigurh stewed together with a generous portion of sad eyes. Better than Flea Bottom brown, but not by much.

Sansa initially thinks Sandor is horrible. Of course, she's right. The Hound is a killer. He is no true knight. Worse, he breaks her porcelain notions of a "true knight" to pieces. Knights are for killing, he tells her. After all, his older brother is a homicidal psychopath. The fact that Gregor has been knighted and cloaked doesn't change anything. If anything, it shows what knights really are. A

80. Arya, meanwhile, is wrestling with her own loss of identity in the House of Black and White. These parallel themes are expressed differently by the Stark girls. Even so, the possibility that one or both will forget their allegiance to the Stark pack sets the stage for their reunion and conflict at Winterfell (show only; season 7).

81. George R. R. Martin, introduction to *Rogues*, edited by George R. R. Martin and Gardner Dozois (New York: Bantam, 2014), 1.

true knight, according to the Hound, is as rare as a real god. "If there are gods," he tells her, "they made sheep so wolves could eat mutton, and they made the weak for the strong to play with" (*Clash* 52, Sansa IV).

Portrait of a Hound: This dog has sad eyes. Do not withhold your love from him. Come closer. That's it . . . there you go. Now admit that you love him. See, now was that so hard? Courtesy of Wikimedia Commons.

It's a terrible thing to tell a child. What he doesn't tell her—at least not directly—is that he still feels like the sheep. He may look and act the predator but he'll always be his brother's mutton chop. As for the gods, well, he's not one for fairytales. But for some reason the religious folk of Westeros feel inclined to care for him. During the Battle of the Blackwater, Sansa prays, "He is no true knight, but he saved me all the same. Save him if you can, and gentle the rage inside him" (*Clash* 57, Sansa v). Like Tormund says: *sad eyes.*

Modern audiences are preconditioned to love the bad boy with a heart of gold. But what would the average, pre-James Dean person think of a man like Sandor Clegane? Keep in mind that the Hound hates his family. He hates his liege lord's family and has no desire to settle down (i.e., not the farming type). Oh, and he likes to kill dudes and isn't shy about saying so (*Clash* 52, Sansa iv).

The Hound is exactly the sort of man that Homer warns us about in the Iliad. A city depends on men of noble character, men who love their clan enough to defend it. But you must be wary of "a clanless, lawless, hearthless man." You can't trust a man who "loves dread strife among his own folk" (*Hom* II 9.64). Aristotle (contrary to Nietzsche on this point) agrees with Homer, "for one by nature unsocial is also a lover of war" (*Pol* 1.1253).[82] The Hound is the worst parts of both criticisms: (1) he does not love his city enough to defend it at the Battle of the Blackwater (wildfire PTSD); (2) he forsakes his clan.

Whether or not the Hound is a lover of war is debatable. What is clear, however, is what both Homer and Aristotle agree is the root of the problem: a hearthless (i.e., rootless) man is a social cancer. The Hound literally curses his king, forsakes his people, and takes to the road.

Martin underscores the condition of the Hound's soul with the name of his horse. "Stranger" is an all-black courser named for the most ominous god of the Seven. This is the God of Death, who ferries souls into the next world. The horse is ill-tempered, and multiple characters

82. On this point, props are due to Petyr Baelish and Bronn. Both men look for war and "dread strife" with the eyes of opportunists. It should be said, however, that both eventually want houses, clans, and all that come with these. They use discord to advance their social station. A good (albeit imperfect) historical analogy here would be Alexander Hamilton.

note that its personality reflects the character of its owner. In keeping with the symbolism, Sandor becomes one of dark Arya's guides. The two talk on and on about death, pigs' feet, death, the fine art of sword-naming, and more death. In a sense, the Hound and his horse will ferry Arya to the other side of her character arc. Or, at least, bring her closer to what her character must become.

Although this chapter isn't the place for a character study on Arya, a word about her influence is needed. The two traveling companions learn to respect each other, and end up changing in small but mutual ways. Arya serves at times as an ethical voice. She also models religious behavior (her nightly devotion to her kill list being the most prominent) on her circuitous pilgrimage to the House of Black and White. In a sense, she is preparing Sandor for his own encounter with religion. But in the end, we think, the Hound will have to find his own way.

Character Study: The Hound

FAN THEORY FUN: CLEGANEBOWL!

CLEGANEBOWL! WHEN YOU hear the blessed word, it will provoke one of two reactions. The first is, "What's a Cleganebowl?" The second is, of course, *"Get hype!"* followed by the sounds of vuvuzelas and hip-hop air horns accompanied by strobing lights. In some cases of especially hyped-up hype, the bass may drop, resulting in imploding earholes and exploding minds. If you're in the set of those having the first reaction, you're frankly missing out on a lot of fun and we need to get you up to speed.

The Cleganebowl theory is elegant in its simplicity. It says that Sandor "the Hound" Clegane will fight his brother, the monstrous, zombified Gregor "the Mountain" Clegane, in a duel to the death.[83] There are several reasons why this bout is so highly anticipated.

83. While we usually give a nod to the originator of fan theories, the Cleganebowl has no temporal origin. It exists (and always has) as fate determined before the dawn of time.

123

First and foremost, many fans think it would make for a great payoff to the character arcs of both men. Sandor—although a chicken-eating killing machine—has become an increasingly pitiable character. The more his backstory is revealed, the more we care about him. He was hideously scarred by his larger, older brother as a child when Gregor held his face to a fiery brazier. Adding a flavor of pointless anguish to Sandor's psyche, Gregor burned his face for the offense of playing with a toy the elder Clegane no longer even wanted. And this was just the start. Sandor grew up watching his older brother rape and slaughter his way to a knighthood, the supposed pinnacle of chivalry and honor in the South.

This of course has left the Hound bitter, angry, and skeptical of the political and religious authorities who legitimized and even celebrated the depraved acts of violence committed by the Mountain. Sandor's hatred for his brother is what drives him. His central motivation is "the hope of seeing his brother's blood upon his blade." This violent fantasy is "all this sad and angry creature lived for" (*Feast* 31, Brienne VI).

The Mountain is portrayed as an unsympathetic monster throughout the series. Gregor was a monster even before he became a *literal* monster. But in typical Martin fashion, he's not just evil for the sake of being evil. The gigantism that gave him his fame also racked his body with intense pain. This includes near-constant and crushing migraine headaches. Rumors suggest that he drinks milk of the poppy the way other men drink wine in an attempt to keep the pain to a dull roar (*Feast* 7, Cersei II). No doubt his infamous temper and cruelty is exacerbated by his suffering and addiction. Death at his brother's hands would be (arguably) an act of mercy as much as vengeance.

The second reason why people typically root for the Cleganebowl is because it promises to be *thunderdomestically awesome.* The two largest, strongest men in the known world, both accomplished and ruthless killers, going at each other with bone-deep hatred and no holds barred promises to be one of the most epic fights in the *Song's* canon. If ever there is a plot point predetermined by the *rule of cool,* this is it.

Unfortunately, when this theory first surfaced it suffered from a mild problem: its two featured subjects were seemingly dead.

But that's where the theory began to take flight. Many sharp-eyed readers drew a connection between (1) the supposed death of the Mountain, (2) the dark human experimentation Qyburn was performing in the black cells of King's Landing, and (3) the massive, hulking, and suspiciously Mountain-shaped new guardian Cersei gets at the end of *Dance,* who never takes his helmet off and thus never reveals his identity. On the screen, the show-runners don't even bother trying to hide this connection, and for good reason. It's rather difficult to hide a gentleman the size of Hafþór Júlíus Björnsson (the actor who plays Gregor)[84] no matter what kind of fancy helm you slap on his head.

That's one half of the 'bowl that's ready for the fight. But what of the Hound? Most readers caught the many, many hints that Sandor wasn't done yet either. The last we see of the Hound, he is alive, though gravely wounded (*Storm* 74, Arya XIII). He is suffering from injuries to his shoulder and leg. Arya says the wounds have become infected and that his eyes shine "bright with fever." He begs her for the mercy of a quick death but she coldly rides away and never looks back. It almost always pays to be suspicious of off-screen deaths.

84. As of the time of writing, the current reigning World's Strongest Man! Now stronger than Magnús Ver Magnússon, even if his name is less memorable and far less magnússy.

The next we hear of the Hound, it seems he's raping and reaving in the Saltpans[85]—or so the rumors say. But this doesn't at all seem like the Hound's style. He's certainly a killer and capable of extreme violence, but "raping and reaving" isn't his modus operandi. Indeed we later find it was the murderous Rorge of the Brave Companions who is responsible for the butchery, after he had also stolen the Hound's helm from Sandor's "grave."

Which leads us to Brienne's attempts to recover Arya and/or Sansa Stark. Brienne gets a tip that one of the girls—if not both—are traveling with the Hound, and tracks him to the Saltpans. There she finds the Quiet Isle, a small island at the mouth of the Trident, and home to silent monks. Their chief mission—in service to the Faith of the Seven—is to bury the dead that frequently float down the Trident. Because, you know, free dead bodies! Brienne meets the Elder Brother, who happens to be quite chatty for the overseer of a silent monastery.[86] He explains that while the Hound did indeed make his way to the isle, he was unable to save him. He later shows Brienne the cairn over Sandor's body as proof.

But close and attentive readers of this chapter noted that the brother is always careful to say that *the Hound* is dead, but that *Sandor* is "at rest." So he apparently draws a distinction between Sandor's outward persona and the man himself. In keeping with this tendency, the brother also explains his own story in similar terms. According to the brother, he was once a warrior, but now that violent man has died and has been reborn as a healer.

Brienne then notices an exceptionally tall member of the community digging graves for the dead. She learns that this silent giant is a novice to the order, moves with a limp, and doesn't speak, on account of his vows. His

85. The Saltpans is a small settlement on the eastern side of Westeros, where the Trident River flows into Crab Bay and then on into the Narrow Sea.

Fan Theory Fun:
CLEGANEBOWL!

86. *Feast* 31, Brienne VI; senior religious leaders at this monastery keep a schedule of speaking days. This schedule is on a weekly rotation.

head is hooded and covered with a scarf, as is customary for the monks.

Simply put, Sandor survived his wounds, was nursed back to health by an exceptionally skilled healer (capable of saving men that are beyond even the maesters' arts), and has found a measure of peace among these monks by attempting to live a quiet life of service. It actually seems quite obvious, once you put it all together.

Again, the show doesn't even bother with this sleight of hand. Arya does indeed leave the Hound for dead. But he pops back up two seasons later, with all the backstory of the Quiet Isle and the Elder Brother carried by the affable Brother Ray (played by Ian McShane). Alas, Brother Ray doesn't last long as a pacifist in Martin's world. He gets about nine minutes of screen time before he's hung from his unfinished sept (S06E07, "The Broken Man"). As a result, Sandor's brief fling with the monastic life is over in less than half an episode and his career as a killing machine resumes. So there you have it: neither Sandor nor Gregor have been deterred by their supposed deaths. They are both alive (so to speak) and on a collision course for Cleganebowl.

The last remaining ingredient for the 'bowl is a bit of plot movement. The Clegane boys just need a reason to fight. Both the books and the series seem to be heading in this direction. If we follow book-only plotlines, Cersei might sidestep her conflict with the Faith Militant with a trial by combat. If so, she could employ her newly animated protector as her champion. If indeed Ser Strong is in Cersei's corner, the Faith of the Seven will need a champion to fight him. And in this corner—*weighing in at seventeen stones of misanthropy*—we give you Sandor "the Hound" Clegane, newly converted champion of the faith.

But this scenario is off the table for the show-only audience. The showrunners delivered the Cleganebowl a nearly fatal blow when King Tommen, under the influence of the pious and hard-nosed High Septon, outlawed trial by combat (S06E08, "No One"). What was once a cacophony of air horns echoing from every online forum and convention hall became a whimper of half-hearted hype.

But then, in a somewhat preposterous series of events, Jon Snow and Daenerys Targaryen sit down for a peace treaty in the ruins of the Dragonpit in King's Landing. Sandor Clegane is among the delegates and he spies the Mountain across the way. Sandor boldly strides up to him, and declares with all the clunky dialogue deep down in his soul, "[This is] not how it ends for you, brother. You know who's coming for you. You've always known" (S07E07, "The Dragon and the Wolf").

Hype for Cleganebowl is officially back on! We can't know under what circumstances the fight may occur, how Sandor will feel about it once it's over, or if the Hound will even survive the bout, but one thing is clear: Sandor has unfinished business with his big brother, undead or no.

Now, there are some who deny the hype. Agnostics will tell you that this isn't a satisfying arc for Sandor. Killing his brother when he has come so close to accepting the power of love, brotherhood, justice, and peace wouldn't make much sense. They may say that we're trading an emotionally satisfying storyline for cheap thrills in a pointless action scene. While we won't deny there is some merit to this way of thinking, to these faithless people we say: *There is no one as accursed as a hypeslayer. All men must hype. What is hype may never die, but rises again hyper and stronger. Sandor is Azor Ahype, confirmed.*
AIR HORNS

Fan Theory Fun: CLEGANEBOWL!

129

BIRD'S-EYE VIEW:
WHY TYRION IS A DICK

The Faithless and the Hound: A Chapter about Our Favorite Skeptics

TYRION IS ACCUSED twice of plotting the murder of a highborn child. The first is Bran Stark (who survives a knife attack) and the second is King Joffrey (regicide by poison). No doubt, Tyrion has done his share of killing. But he's not a child-killer. So why is he a magnet for this accusation?

The simple bird's-eye view answer for this is that Martin has modeled Tyrion after Richard III (1452–1485 CE). Richard III was briefly king during the War of the Roses and is rumored to have "disappeared" two boys (Edward V and Richard of York). Both boys were sons of King Edward IV and—after a brief stint as king by the older son—declared to be illegitimate because of the marital impropriety of their parents (in this case, bigamy). Whether, why, or how the boys were murdered is of little importance from a literary perspective. Martin is far more interested in the rumors.

Indeed, the rumors about Richard III are too interesting to ignore. He was said to have a number of maladies (probably erroneously). Depending on the propaganda, he was short, hunched, twisted of spine, with a limp arm, etc. Shakespeare borrows from some of these rumors. For medieval storytellers, disabilities can be literary devices used to reflect a villain's inner demons. Martin explains:

> *I love Richard III. He's one of my favorite historical characters. He wasn't a hunchback. He didn't have a twisted arm. But he was the king that was deposed by Henry VII. So the Tudor historians tried to make him a physically twisted, deceitful, kinslay-*

ing, child-slaying monster. And a lot of what happened to Richard III is happening to Tyrion. Tyrion is someone who is easily cast as a villain. The dwarf, hated by the gods, so they twisted his body into unfortunate shapes. This is a clear sign of the evil inside him. This is how the medieval mindset worked.[87]

87. "Real History behind Game of Thrones: Part One," YouTube, November 16, 2017.

*Bird's-Eye View:
Why Tyrion Is a Dick*

So there can be no doubt that Tyrion is meant to parallel Richard in a few ways. But Martin's outcomes for such characters are rarely predictable. And, of course, Martin takes such histories and infuses them with fantasy.

Coin Featuring Richard III: Obverse of silver groat from 1483. Courtesy of Wikimedia Commons.

Martin is known for taking well-known fantasy figures and putting his own signature on them. His world has giants, dragons, and shadow creatures. And if we look close enough, we'll find his take on werewolves, dryads, and frost giants. Tyrion may be Martin's most compelling adaptation. He is a dwarf living in a world that is highly suspicious (and sometimes loathsome) of disability. Tyrion is Martin's answer to the question: What would it be like to be a dwarf in a world that believes that disability is a mark of divine hatred? In this way, he takes a well-known fantasy trope—*the wealthy and self-interested dwarf*—and infuses it with medieval realism.

Crueler Gods

DEMIGODS BEYOND THE WALL

6

Good fences make cold neighbors.

—ROBERT BIFRÖST

Distinctive Elements
- ritualized covenants
- child sacrifice
- icy hubris monsters

Key Adherents
- Craster
- Gilly
- The Night King
- The Night's King (yeah, it's confusing)

TRAVEL GUIDE

WHILE THERE IS a long-standing travel advisory issued from the Night's Watch, life in the "Truth North" can be quite liberating. Leave the hustle and bustle of the kingsroad behind and experience the rustic charm of snowy solitude. Lovers exchanging vows will find stunning crimson foliage in the godswood, even in winter. But adventurers beyond the Wall will find few bed and breakfast options. Craster's Keep—a family-run hostel—is a popular sojourn. Reviews on Craster's hospitality, however, are mixed.

Tourists will find a dearth of lavatory facilities in the True North. If your ranger has brought a shovel, local etiquette expects you will dig a hole for your night soil.

(Digging will be the duty of your portly, well-read steward.) If the traveler has need to make water, a discreet tree may prove useful. Tourists should take care to avoid making water on or near a Heart Tree. If the trunk features the carving of a human face, prayer is welcomed, whereas urination is frowned upon.

Once among the trees, avoid pale men with blue eyes. Not only will these Aryans render the climate uncomfortably brisk, they are known to recruit unsuspecting tourists for their army of the dead. They do, on occasion, stroll by without event. Even so, they are not much for conversation and speak only in pretentious shrieks.

DEEP DIVE: FEAR THE FROST

ONE OF THE most puzzling *Ice and Fire* mysteries is the motivation of the White Walkers. The "Others" are the first and worst antagonists we meet in *A Game of Thrones*. But while we know how deadly they are, do we really know what they want? *To zombify every last person on the Planetos? To holiday in Dorne for a bit of tan-line work?* The personality of Martin's most daunting antagonist—the Night King—is almost entirely veiled. As this book was written in the Long Night of Martin's authorial brain freeze, we're just groping in the dark for answers. But unlike Jon Snow, we do know a few things, and our goal here is to overanalyze them until hell freezes over.

The Others are reminiscent of the Jötnar (frost giants) of Norse mythology. In the most basic terms, the frost giants live at the world's edge, beyond a wall designed to keep them out. Or, in the words of super-nerd Norsologist Neil Gaiman:

> *The world is a flat disk, and the sea encircles the perimeter. Giants live at the edges of the world, beside the deepest seas. To keep the giants at bay, Odin and Vili and Ve made a wall.*[88]

88. Neil Gaiman, *Norse Mythology* (New York: Norton, 2017), 33.

Don't let the reference to giants fool you: in Norse mythology, Jötnar (plural for Jötunn) are not necessarily supersized.[89] While "giants" is a legitimate translation of Jötnar, it could just as easily mean "gluttons." This isn't a bad way to think about the White Walkers: they are winter demigods that consume. In the same way that winter consumes the landscape in the North, the Others are on the warpath to consume the children of summer.

89. The word derives from Old Norse *etall*, which means "consuming" (compare also Old Norse *iotunn* and Danish *jætte*).

When the Stark men repeat their mantra that "winter is coming," the reader knows that this includes the Night King and his freaky fellows. In other words, we shouldn't draw neat lines between gods and the elemental forces of nature. In Norse cosmology, these lines are blurred. Indeed, the entire universe was constructed from the body parts of the first giant, Ymir.

> *Odin and his brothers [the patricidal sons of Ymir] made the soil from Ymir's flesh. Ymir's bones they piled up into mountains and cliffs. . . . Look up into the sky: you are looking at the inside of Ymir's skull. . . . And the clouds you see by day? These were once Ymir's brains, and who knows what thoughts they are thinking, even now.*[90]

90. Gaiman, *Norse Mythology*, 32–33.

In this creation myth, the frost giants—like all of nature—are born from Ymir's body. (And yes, the reference to "brain clouds" really hit us in the old *Joe Versus the Volcano* nostalgia-bone, too.) The Jötnar are not themselves elemental forces, but they are of like kin. While it's impossible to know Ymir's thoughts, it's not difficult to predict what his children will do. They are as predicable as the seasons.

This is where Martin's evil genius is most interesting. He seems to have borrowed bits and pieces from Norse mythology but removed all predictable outcomes. Even the seasons cannot be predicted in Martin's universe. Even so, the Jötnar parallel may provide one possible answer to the question of character motivation.

Given the Night King's unnaturally long life and superhuman abilities, he functions as a demigod. Indeed, some characters in the story speak of the Others as gods. Craster—worst father/husband ever—ritually sacrifices his infant sons to the Others. The Night King doesn't eat the children (as one might expect from gluttonous demigods); rather, he frosts them over like the Coors Light ice train. After the Silver Bullet Express pulls through, the boys become cutesy White Walkers, presumably with lifespans like the Jötnar or dark elves (able to be killed but not to die of old age). As such, these demigods don't consume children as much as they consume the entire landscape of the living.

The Night King seems to have supernatural command over the dead and the weather, and he is all but immortal. If this doesn't demonstrate divinity, we don't know what does. Indeed, Jeor Mormont speaks of the White Walkers in divine terms when he refers to them as "crueler gods" (S02E03, "What Is Dead May Never Die"). Not only does this monstrous character function as a deity, he is among the most powerful.

✤ Excursus: Lesser-Known Gods of the North ✤

Osha tells Bran that the Old Gods are her gods, too. She also claims that beyond the Wall, they are the only gods (So1E08, "The Pointy End"). This is not entirely accurate, according to Maester Yandel. Yandel mentions a handful of different gods worshipped in remote regions. For example, the clans of Storrold's Point are rumored to worship crab gods (*World,* "The Wildlings"). We'll just assume that this is a frigid but free-love nude beach until Martin corrects us.

Yandel concedes that these are only rumors, but one of his notes is interesting considering what we know of Craster's theology. Yandel refers to "dark gods beneath the ground in the Frostfangs." He also mentions "gods of snow and ice on the Frozen Shore." Could either of these be references to the Others? The White Walkers are certainly known for their command of snow and ice and the label "dark gods" is justifiable.

One other point to consider: Osha tells Maester Luwin that the Others are not gone; they've only been sleeping (S01E07, "You Win or You Die"). Could it be that they were dormant beneath or beyond the Frostfangs in the "Lands of Always Winter"? If Osha is right on this point, a religion created to honor the White Walkers might easily be described as one that worships "dark gods beneath the ground in the Frostfangs."

Crueler Gods: Demigods beyond the Wall

At the risk of redundancy and annoyance, we're arguing that there are indeed gods within Martin's world. Some we see and some we don't. The Others are a case in point for functional demigods. When interviewed about his fantasy religions, Martin has said,

> *I don't think any gods are likely to be showing up in Westeros, any more than they already do. We're not going to have one appearing,* deus ex machina, *to affect the outcomes of things, no matter how hard anyone prays.*[91]

Without parsing his words too finely, two of his phrases are especially interesting. (1) ... *any more than they already do.* So if there's going to be any divine intervention, the divine agent is already in the story. (2) ... *deus ex machina.* This Latin phrase literally means "a god from a machine." It comes from Greek and Roman theater set design. (If a god was lowered down by crane onto the stage of a play, this was a *deus ex machina.*) In literary terms, it simply means that some god you've never met before in the story shows up to resolve the plot, usually in a sudden or contrived way. In Martin's world, this means that the Black Goat of Qohor won't be descending from the clouds.

Martin's answer also suggests that the gods already introduced will be the only gods we meet in *A Song of Ice and Fire.* The most simple solution here is that the Others and the Targaryen dragons are the crucial elemental forces/demigods.[92] They are not "divine" in a Judeo-Christian sense but they are definitely "giants" in a Norse sense.

91. Anders, "George R. R. Martin Explains," io9.com, July 21, 2011.

92. R'hllor is a bit trickier and will be discussed elsewhere. Relax, we *got* this.

The Murder of Ymir: This drawing by Lorenz Frølich
(ca. 19th c.) depicts Ymir's murder by his sons: Odin, Vili,
and Ve. Courtesy of Wikimedia Commons.

A common refrain among fans is that most of the
Westerosi chessboard is a squabble among pawns. Once
most of the pawns have been spent, we'll see the dragons
move northward and the Others move southward. This
would make the clash between the Mother of Dragons and
the Night King the strategic climax of the *Song of Ice and
Fire.* With this in mind, we can measure the motives of the
Mother of Dragons, and Martin helpfully places Daenerys
in his story as a point-of-view character. But what moti-

vates the Night King? One possible interpretation of the Night King's intentions draws from his origin story.

According to the showrunners, the original White Walker was once human. Over ten thousand years before the Baratheon period, he was transformed into a weapon to be used against human invaders. In order to battle human colonization, the magic-wielding "Children" weaponized a man by transforming him into a demigod. Once created, the Night King was able to create others like himself and raise an army of the dead. In this version of the story, the Night King functions as the god of death. In the same way that death must come to all mortals, the Night King must bring winter to Westeros.[93]

93. This describes show-only events (S06E05, "The Door").

94. S03E03, "Walk of Punishment"; Mance Rayder observes the elaborate swirl patterns formed of dismembered men and horses, and grimly observes, "Always the artists."

That said, we know that the White Walkers have a culture. They have language. They have a system of symbols that is evidence of writing at least on par with the First Men.[94] They use technology, wear clothes, have a social hierarchy, and perform rituals. Also, the Night King isn't a programmed automaton. He commands troops, employs strategy, and accepts gifts. The Night King is more like a Cameronesque Terminator with Mr. Freeze gumption (*"Whad Keeeeled de dinosaurs? De ahce age!"*) In the same way that the gods of Martin's imagination lack clear motive or predictability, the Night King's personality remains a cultic cryptogram.

This brings us to one of the central truths of Martin's cosmology. In this world, gods and monsters are indistinguishable. Martin's gods do not have discernable personalities, and may well function as weapons of mass destruction. Even when these supernatural elements accept covenants with mortals, they ultimately lack literary empathy. In short, they are powerful and can indeed intercede in human affairs but they are not "personal" in the way that those who pray to them imagine.

HISTORICAL BACKDROP:
SUZERAIN-VASSAL TREATIES

ANCIENT POLITICAL ARRANGEMENTS involving blessings, obedience, military service, etc., were common in the ancient world. One form of this was the suzerain-vassal covenant. In this form of treaty, a more powerful chieftain (called the *suzerain,* or feudal lord) made a deal with the chieftain of a lesser tribe (called the *vassal*), trading protection for allegiance and service. Think of almost every prison movie you've seen and you've basically got it. But in the ancient world, the covenant between more powerful and less powerful tribes called upon the witness of the gods and detailed a litany of curses if either party breached the contract.

One example of this kind of covenant is the Treaty of Esarhaddon. Esarhaddon was a king of the Neo-Assyrian Empire (ca. 680–669 BCE). In this covenant, the lesser tribe agrees to be devoted to the prince, honor the line of succession of Esarhaddon's family, honor the territories of Assyria, etc. But the key point of the covenant was to give the lesser tribe protection. In exchange, Esarhaddon (and son) got tribute and obedience from the vassal. All this was agreed to as an oath before "Aššur, Father of the Gods." It is highly likely that the Israelites of this period borrowed the idea of a written covenant from these suzerain-vassal covenants. Hence, the seeds of the book of Deuteronomy— the fifth book of the Bible—were planted.

If Deuteronomy (the book, not the cat) took shape in the shadow of the Neo-Assyrian Empire, it was composed when the Assyrian king would have expected allegiance from the Israelites, specifically the tribes of Judah. But instead of a covenant with the Assyrian king, Deuteronomy details a new kind of covenant. Israel bypassed their natural suzerain and created a covenant with a deity. In short, the book is a rejection of the Assyrian king. *We don't need your protection and we refuse to obey you or give you tribute. We've found a bigger and better (divine) suzerain.* This was an unprecedented political move in the history of the ancient Near East.

Against this backdrop, it's easy to see suzerain-vassal treaties all over Westeros. The most powerful suzerain (at least officially) is House Baratheon. The rest of the Seven Kingdoms are the vassals. In the North, the Starks function as the suzerain in covenants with the vassal Glovers, Karstarks, Manderlys, etc. Now consider this: what if a member of the Seven Kingdoms wanted to shun the realm of kings, lines of succession, and tributes? What if a tribal leader wanted to strike a deal directly with the gods and pay tribute directly to them? This appears to be exactly what Craster has done north of the Wall.

Of course, Craster's a total doucherocket and nobody deserves to be compared to him. But we're not talking about his family values; the comparison is very limited. Our point is simply that we have a precedent in the ancient world for the sort of covenant that Craster has with the Others. Finally, it should be pointed out that the Israelites of this period were in the process of rejecting not only covenants with foreign kings, but also rejecting the practice of incest and child sacrifice (e.g., Leviticus 18). So, in this sense, Craster may function as an anti-Abraham or anti-Moses figure.

CHARACTER STUDY: GILLY

C RASTER'S ENCLAVE HAS a few key markers of a religious cult. It is authoritarian, secretive, isolated from larger society, and emphasizes beliefs/practices that seem unorthodox to outsiders. There can be no doubt that Craster is a true believer. He has a pact with the Others that he thinks makes him a godly man. In addition, outsiders are altogether repulsed by Craster's sexual behavior. The showrunners lean into this with gusto: after a baby boy is born, the women chant *gift the to gods* until the ritual child sacrifice is offered. There is absolutely no reason to doubt their commitment to Sparkle Motion.

To label it a "cult," however, is a problem for three reasons. The first is that the word is vague in popular usage; it's usually just an imprecise insult. The second is that a more precise study would look for features of behavior control, information control, thought control, and emotional control.[95] We just don't know enough about Craster's family to look for these features (although behavior control is clearly employed). The third is that the book's portrayal of Craster's wives doesn't emphasize mind control. Which, of course, leads us to Gilly.

Gilly (Craster's daughter and youngest wife) doesn't present as a programmed devotee to a religious movement. What is even more telling is that she doesn't seem to require "deprogramming" after she escapes Craster's Keep. Her driving motivation is her son's survival, and this remains constant. Aside from her growing affection for Sam, Gilly's character doesn't undergo much of a liberating transformation. This is in keeping with her portrayal in the books. In Martin's vision, at least a few of Craster's wives (Gilly's mother included) are decidedly

95. For more, see the synopsis of Steven Hassan's BITE model, at freedomofmind.com/bite-model/.

against Craster's covenant. These women aren't religious kooks in the books; they are enslaved. They lament the loss of their sons and convince Sam to take Gilly and her boy south (*Storm* 33, Samwell 11). The show, therefore, follows Martin's lead with Gilly's character but changes the religious context of her upbringing.

So we are left with two different portraits of Craster's Keep: the show gives us a Kool-Aid-drinking culture; the books give us an oppressively religious husband and subversive wives. Gilly's character makes better sense, we think, in the books' context. But regardless of context, both Martin and the showrunners agree that Gilly is morally aware and willing to resist authority. For a historical analogy, Gilly is like Sarah Pratt, one of the earliest whistle-blowers on the Mormonite practice of plural marriage and sexual harassment.[96]

It's not that Gilly is unimpressed with the power of the gods. After all, she fears the Others enough to run for her life. But she views the gods' power in terms of territory. Both she and her mother think that escaping to the South will put them out of reach. This idea of divinity is similar to early forms of henotheism, which thought that different gods had different regional jurisdictions.[97]

Gilly expresses this view when she is literally shipping herself with Sam. After their "boat sex," Sam is feeling guilty because he's broken his Night's Watch vow of celibacy. He confesses that he said his vows under a Heart Tree. Gilly observes that they are at sea; no tree god is likely to see what they've done on a boat (*Feast* 35, Samwell IV). The authority of the gods, in her view, is linked to their territory. Sam is being silly.

Territory is also a problem for Gilly's well-being in the HBO version of her story. No doubt, fleeing to the South saves her. But her time with the prostitutes of Mole's

96. The earlier Latter-Day Saints (i.e., less latter than they are today) called themselves "Mormonites." We've kept the archaic title here to avoid besmirching contemporary Mormons.

97. Adherents of henotheism (also called monolatry) usually worshipped one god, but granted that other gods deserve worship by peoples of other tribes. Gilly, of course, doesn't fall neatly into this category, because she doesn't worship any single god. However, her notion of divine territory does indeed fit within this worldview. Osha (also from the True North) says something along these lines when she tells Bran that the old gods have no power in the South (So1E08, "The Pointy End"). *How can the Heart Trees see in the South when—having been cut down—they no longer have eyes?*

Town and with Sam's family is alienating and dangerous. Gilly, in essence, is a refugee. And Sam is a reluctant and indecisive guide who is only slowly learning to find his courage. We will have to wait and see whether the people of the South are any less cruel than the gods of the North.

FAN THEORY FUN:
THE ABOMINABLE CROW MAN

L ET US SPIN you a tale that may or may not shed light on the agenda of the White Walkers. It is a story of war, peace, a covenantal crow, and glacier-sized speculation.[98] As a certain desert-dwelling hermit once said, much depends on your point of view.

Our story begins with the Night's King—and we'll let you decide how this archetypal crow relates to the so-called "Night King" of the White Walkers.[99] Much of our information about the legendary figure comes from the tales Old Nan used to tell Bran to both frighten and fascinate the young lord (*Storm* 24, Bran IV). Long ago, the thirteenth Lord Commander of the Night's Watch, who is said to have been a Stark, peered over the icy Wall and beheld a vision of great beauty. He saw a woman who had skin "as white as the moon" and eyes like "blue stars." Venturing beyond the Wall, he found her irresistible, even though her touch was cold as ice. As Nan tells it (because she's gross) the Night's King gave her his seed and his soul. He then bound the Black Brothers to this mysterious woman using dark sorcery.

This is when our man became a king in earnest. He ruled as a tyrant from the Night Fort, the oldest and largest of the nineteen fortresses along the Wall. As the years rolled by, the Night's King dominated the North. In an effort to take him down, an alliance was forged between

98. We normally like to credit a specific fan or group of fans wherever credit is due. The origin of this fan theory is especially difficult to track down, however. This is an old theory (or an amalgamation of several old theories) that we haven't been able to source. It is possible that some of these musings got started on AOL message boards during the Age of Heroes.

99. For a quick gloss, the *Night King* (no possessive "s") is the leader of the White Walkers, whereas the *Night's King* is an ancient member of the Night's Watch who became Lord Commander and then hooked up with a cold-stone-foxy cougar beyond the Wall. It takes a bit of mental gymnastics to say they are one and the same. But then again, all the best Valyrian foilsmiths are excellent mental gymnasts.

an ancient Stark King of Winter—Brandon "the Breaker" Stark—and Joramun, the "King Beyond the Wall." They rallied their respective bannermen and wildlings, and formed a hammer-and-anvil campaign from north and south. Thus ended the rule of the soul-sowing spouse.

The two conquering kings discovered that the fallen Lord Commander had been offering child sacrifices to the Others. As in most ancient cultures, hybrid creatures (like the offspring of a lordly crow and an ice deity) are considered abominations. These chilling hybrids presumably helped to populate the Others.[100] Horrified, Kings Bran and Joramun struck the name of the Night's King from the lists of the Black Brothers. His name was both forbidden and forgotten.[101]

This story has fueled fan speculation about what, if any, significance the Night's King has to the plot of *A Song of Ice and Fire*. Specifically, what can it tell us about the origins and motivations of the White Walkers? Perhaps the surviving Black Brothers under the Night's King fled northward, eventually becoming wights under the control of the White Walkers, if not becoming Others themselves. Some have keyed into the fact that the Night's King hooked up with a woman who appeared to be an Other herself. If so, maybe there are half-man, half-Other hybrids haunting the forests beyond the Wall.

Before going further, we ought to acknowledge that it's notoriously difficult to sift fact, myth, and legend with ancient history. This is no less true in Westeros. The people in Martin's world struggle to understand their history and prehistory, and without modern archaeology and carbon dating to aid them. Making matters worse, ancient minds tended to use historical events and numbers symbolically.

Jon Snow became the 998th Lord Commander of the Night's Watch. How exciting! Will something special happen with the 1000th? It's such a nice, round number,

100. For example, the hybrid creatures called "nephilim" in Genesis 6:1-4 are the source of all sorts of evil in later historical fictions. They are the offspring of the "sons of God" and the "daughters of men." Some texts call them "giants.".

101. This is an echo of the Roman tradition of removing names from historical memory: *damnatio memoriae*.

maybe it has prophetic significance! *Not so fast,* says Samwell Tarly, proto-maester and robust reader. Sam's pored over the records, searched through the annals, crunched the numbers, and can account for only 674 Lord Commanders (*Feast* 15, Samwell II).

Sam goes on to state that the maesters of the Citadel openly question *all* of their history. After all, Westerosi history includes credibility-stretching tales of kings who lived lifespans of hundreds of years and heroic knights who lived thousands of years before the Andals brought the concept of knighthood to the shores of Westeros. In fact, everything they think they know about the Long Night, the creation of the Wall, and the Age of Heroes comes from the writings of septons who lived thousands of years after the supposed events took place.

All this is to say that we don't really have any reason to trust the details of these legends, but if we take the basic facts of the myth, inject what we know of Westerosi culture, and heed the words of Master Kenobi, we might be able to see other possibilities.

What if the gist of the Night's King story is right but the details and motivations are lost to time? What if this tale is an explanation for how the war against the Others was settled? And if so, are we justified in reframing the Night's King as a kind of peacemaker between the tribes of Men, the Children, and the Others? Maybe the Abominable Crow Man was a necessary bridge to a covenant.

Legend says that Bran the Builder constructed the Wall, but there are many reasons to doubt it. If you compare the other works of the ancient Stark architect (Starkitect, if you will)—Winterfell and Storm's End—they're on a completely different scale from the Wall. They are both impressive fortifications, to be sure. Winterfell is especially tricked out: greenhouses to grow fruits and vegetables during even the coldest winters, geothermal

Fan Theory Fun: The Abominable Crow Man

147

heating, and an impressive underground necropolis. But it certainly doesn't feature seven hundred-foot-high walls that magically repel the undead.

To state the obvious, we know the Others are associated with ice: their speech is described as the harsh and cracking sound of ice shattering and breaking, and they use weapons and armor that appear to be formed out of ice. Add to this the horrifying legend that they ride *large ice spiders* and it's pretty clear who wields the ice magic in this world. If anyone has the power to construct a magic ice wall in Martin's world, it's the Others. Perhaps, then, the Wall was constructed as a demilitarized zone between the two factions. *You stay on your side, and we'll stay on ours.*

In the cultures of the First Men, the Andals, the Rhoynar, the Dothraki, and the cities of Slaver's Bay, marriage alliances are an important part of forging and maintaining peace. In this scenario, the Night's King is transformed from a horny warlock to a dutiful Stark prince, serving humankind by wedding the daughter of a high-ranking Other. The marriage alliance solidifies rule from a central fortification along the Wall, keeping the peace and maintaining the DMZ for arbitration of disputes.

Such a covenant is also consistent with how the First Men made peace with the Children of the Forest. *We'll promise to stop cutting down your sacred trees, and let you have the dark forests, caves, and grottoes you love so much; just give us the streams and fields.* With this strict division of territory and the promise to stay out of each other's way came peace, and eventually shared worship (i.e., a covenant). If only the Andals had kept the deal, we might have more than a handful of Children left in small enclaves north of the Wall. (Their fancy fireball magic would be particularly handy against the highly flammable armies of the Others.)

We know why men would want to have a wall protecting themselves from the Others, but why would the Others need protection from the men? There are certainly things that men possess or historically have possessed that could strike fear into their ice-cold hearts. Obsidian, Valyrian steel, dragons, fire magic, torches—all are mortal threats to beings who appear to be made of wicker furniture and kerosene.[102]

From the Others' perspective, the men are in breach of the long-standing peace. The Children are close to extinction. Men in the form of wildlings now number in the hundreds of thousands north of the Wall, violating the Other's sovereign territory. And the Night's Watch regularly sends ranging parties to harass their lands.

This new point of view allows us to consider the events beyond the Wall during the Baratheon period in a new light. In response to human aggression, the Others make the strategic decision to send a warning. They target and kill some of the interlopers, allowing one to survive and bring the warning south. In essence, what looks like ritualized murder is the message: *Back off, honor your agreements, or else.* Of course, by the Baratheon period, no person south of the Wall remembers the original pact or understands the significance of the warning. The Night's Watch responds by sending the largest ranging party north of the Wall in living memory. Meanwhile, worshippers of R'hllor have begun landing on the shores of Westeros, with an explicit mission of defeating the forces of ice and darkness with their fire and light. Dragons have suddenly reentered the world. If this theory holds water, Martin's chief conflict is a bit like the Cuban Missile Crisis. Neither party actually *wants* war, but there are outright provocations on both sides and even more misunderstandings that lead to escalation. Unfortunately, neither the humans nor

102. The following quote by Queen Alysanne (an early Westerosi dragonlord) is revealing. Archmaester Gyldayn reports that Alysanne's dragon refused to fly over the Wall. This might suggest that the Wall's magic works to keep fire magic in the South. In Alysanne's words, "Thrice I flew Silverwing high above Castle Black, and thrice I tried to take her north beyond the Wall . . . but every time she veered back south again and refused to go. Never before has she refused to take me where I wished to go. I laughed about it when I came down again, so the black brothers would not realize anything was amiss, but it troubled me then and it troubles me still." Pre-publication excerpt provided by George R. R. Martin, "A Fire & Blood Excerpt Just For You!" Not a Blog, September 27, 2018.

the Others have a Khrushchev or a Kennedy to de-escalate the situation.

We know Westeros has no shortage of prophecy and portents. Perhaps the White Walkers have their share, too. They see the same red comet in the heavens, they know that dragons are returning; perhaps they have an inverse "Prince That Was Promised" prophecy and are nervously eyeing the ascent of Jon and/or Daenerys. Dany had visions of riding a dragon above an army "armored all in ice" that she "melts away like the dew" (*Storm* 23, Daenerys 11). Perhaps the Others have their share of frightening visions, increasing their defensiveness and state of alarm.

Which brings us to Craster, that freaky Freefolk father who likes to keep things all in the family north of the Wall. Craster (godly man that he is) has been offering his children to the Others for countless years. He is said to be the bastard son of a disgraced Black Brother and a wildling woman, which makes him something of a North/South hybrid. It's quite possible that at this point in the story, he is the last remaining man to give children as tribute to the Others. Could Craster's murder—resulting in the end to sacrificial offerings—mark the end of the covenant between humans and Others?

We know from the *Game of Thrones* series that the White Walkers seem to reproduce by magically transforming men into Others.[103] When the treacherous Black Brothers mutinied at Craster's Keep, they simultaneously ended the ritual of peace offerings and cut off the White Walkers' means of reproduction.[104] In light of this, could it be more than coincidence that from this point the Others begin amassing an army, marching on the Wall, and ultimately breaching it?

The shortcomings of this theory are fairly obvious. One, it's a *lot* of speculation, even for the type of tinfoil-

Crueler Gods: Demigods beyond the Wall

103. S04E04, "Oathkeeper"; compare also the origin of the show's Night King in S06E05, "The Door."

104. It is also noteworthy that the murderous crows violated the holy practice of guest right, which is as binding upon the guest as it is the host. As we discuss elsewhere in this book, guest right is seen as sacred; a violation of it would be an affront to the gods. The Others may very well *be* gods, or at least connected to the "old gods" and their magic.

hat-wearing fan-theorizing that we're willing to traffic in. And the television series seems to make explicit the origins and motivations of the Others as living bioweapons the Children created as a last-ditch effort in their war against the First Men, one that they later lost control of. So maybe the Others have no motive or drive beyond their all-consuming quest to destroy humanity.

However, as we've seen time and time again, the showrunners do not always fully reveal the underlying book plots. The show is forced to simplify and streamline characters, motivations, and entire plotlines to be something one could actually film within a reasonable time frame and budget. Interestingly, there even might have been hints to this internal divide between Weiss, Benioff, and Martin. When the episode "Oathkeeper" initially aired, and we got to see the first glimpse of the character that we will eventually come to know as the Night King, HBO's behind-the-scenes information labeled this figure as the "Night's King," causing many fans to speculate eagerly on the connection between him and the ill-fated thirteenth Lord Commander. A day later, HBO changed the reference to the generic term "White Walker." Since then, Martin has refused to answer questions about how the two characters are related, only saying, "As for the Night's King (the form I prefer), in the books he is a legendary figure, akin to Lann the Clever and Brandon the Builder, and no more likely to have survived to the present day than they have."[105]

Finally, Martin has said many times that there are no characters in his books that are purely good or purely evil, not even excepting notoriously heinous individuals such as Ramsay Snow/Bolton or the infamous Greyjoy brothers Euron and Victarion. So it is perplexing that the biggest badasses of the series, the White Walkers, are reduced in the show to something like Terminators

Fan Theory Fun: The Abominable Crow Man

105. "So Spake Martin" archive, westeros.org/Citadel/SSM/Entry/12392.

run amok. It could be that Martin doesn't see the Others as characters at all, but more as elemental forces of the world, or manifestations of gods. The concept of good or evil would apply to them as much as a forest fire or a hurricane. But it would be in line with the showrunners' track record to simplify Martin's labyrinthine plot. So in service to time and budget, the show treats the Others as out-of-control technology and gives us more time with the political intrigue of the Seven Kingdoms. If so, this explanation keeps alive the possibility that in the books the White Walkers' motivations are much more complex. It may be that the realms of men are as much to blame for the conflict as the mysterious Others.

At least, from a certain point of view.

BIRD'S-EYE VIEW:
MACUMBER BLINKS

WE MAY HEAR an echo of the Ymir creation myth in Old Nan's story about Macumber (show only). According to her story, the sky is blue because humans live inside of an eye of a blue-eyed giant named Macumber (S01E03, "Lord Snow"). The myth is repeated by Oberyn Martell (S04E03, "Breaker of Chains"). In both cases, the story is used as an example of extreme absurdity with no foundation in reality.

But what if Old Nan's story is a literary device? According to the Norse creation myth, the great wall is made from Ymir's eyelashes. "To keep the giants at bay, Odin and Vili and Ve made a wall from Ymir's eyelashes and set it around the middle of the world. They called the place within the wall Midgard."[106]

106. Gaiman, *Norse Mythology*, 33.

Our suggestion is more absurd than compelling, but you've read this far: *What if Ymir's eyelash-wall falls?* Or, in other words: *What if Macumber blinks?* We'll get the show's answer to that question in season 8.

152

Breaking the Wheel

MARTIN'S MESSIAHS

7

*If liberty and equality, as is thought by some, are chiefly to
be found in democracy, they will be best attained when all
persons alike share in government to the utmost.*

—ARISTOTLE

Distinctive Elements

- cults of personality
- egalitarianism
- vague prophetic portents
- boat sex

Key Adherents

- Jon Snow
- Daenerys Targaryen

TRAVEL GUIDE

THE WALL LEFT you cold, King's Landing is just
too uptight, and the Dothraki Sea is far too rustic.
If adventure and mystery are what you seek, a
cruise to the Smoking Sea is in order. Encounter the Doom
of Valyria with all of its old-world charm. The shattered
subcontinent's haunted coastlines and boiling waters have
provided a worthy challenge to adventurous seafarers for
centuries.

Dozens of volcanoes and dark, angry skies await you
in the smoldering remains of the Valyrian peninsula! Hike
the ruins of Valyria, and experience firsthand the culture

of the Stone Men. Be sure to bring hand sanitizer. Trace the footsteps of the doomed Gerion Lannister expedition. Perhaps you'll be the one to find the Lannisters' long-lost ancestral blade, Brightroar, and countless other treasures and artifacts left over from before the Doom. Experience the *literal* magic of Old Valyria today!

CHARACTER STUDIES:
DANY AND JON

STORIES THAT GROW from sacred ground are usually saturated with typology. The story of Jesus casts him as a Moses-type. Luther, at times, is a Paul-type. Pope Francis is a self-styled St. Francis of Assisi-type. Bing Bong is a Christ-type. And so the circle of typology goes. The great literary scholar Northrop Frye was convinced that students of Shakespeare would never fully appreciate the playwright without understanding biblical typology.[107] Even Tolkien, who intentionally avoided biblical allegory, is not immune to creation myths, prophetic poetry, demonic adversaries, and resurrections.

It stands to reason, then, that Martin—who is highly interested in religious worldbuilding—does not exist in a typological vacuum. One or more of his characters is going to parallel Jesus: prophesied as divinely appointed royalty; escapes death as an infant from an evil king; and fathered by a surrogate parent. One or more of Martin's characters will be betrayed, killed, and raised from the dead. We shouldn't be surprised if one or more of Martin's characters is a Moses-type: the liberator of slaves and the founder of a new form of governance.

Martin also includes minor echoes of biblical mythology that give us a glimpse into the worldview(s) of ancient peoples. For example, a great event in the sky—

107. Frye makes the same claim of English literature more broadly too, argument that "a student of English literature who does not know the Bible does not understand a good deal of what is going on in what (s)he reads: the most conscientious student will be continually misconstruing the implications, even the meaning." See *The Great Code: The Bible and Literature* (New York: Harcourt Brace Jovanovich Pardes Ilana, 1982), x.

in this case, a comet—is interpreted as an omen (*Clash* 8, Tyrion 11). The most famous example of this type of thing in the ancient world is the star that leads the magi to Jesus in Matthew's Gospel. Martin uses minor biblical echoes like this for worldbuilding rather than to create a one-to-one correlation. So we'll try to refrain from getting literary boners over such minor details when we find them.[108] Rather, we'll focus on two major characters who look like they've been shaped by biblical typology. To be specific, we'll point out the messianic typologies of Daenerys Targaryen and Jon Snow (yes, we know the show revealed that Jon's real name is actually Aegon VI. But he'll always be Jon Snow to us. We'll also accept Aemon, *George*).

Dany and Jon are on trajectories to the Iron Throne. Both begin as highly unlikely claimants, only to be revealed as heirs of the Targaryen line. The lives of Dany and Jon show a number of parallel events, including gaining acceptance from foreign tribes and losing lovers to untimely deaths. But the most compelling parallels between their narrative arcs—*those that motivate their political decisions*—are messianic.

By calling them types of messiahs, we're appealing to the concept broadly. We're thinking broadly enough so that both Moses (the messianic prototype) and Jesus (the messianic antitype) are relevant. We are *not* suggesting that Martin had any particular biblical character or story in mind. But once recognized, these parallels show a pattern. And Martin is not immune to literary patterns. In truth, he traffics in literary types like cartel, mule, and distributor all rolled into a single intertextual inkslinger.

108. When studying types we must avoid drinking our own Kool-Aid. For example, after liberating the Ghiscari slaves, Daenerys is called "mhysa." In the Ghiscari language this means *mother*, but in several Semitic languages, this word sounds like "Moses." This is the sort of loose connection that probably means nothing. And even if this title is a wink to Moses typology, we might just as easily point to Harriet "Moses" Tubman. Tubman—who also literally walked slaves to freedom—was called both "Moses" and "mother" by her contemporaries. Further down the rabbit hole, we should also note that the word "mhysa" also sounds like "messiah" in Hebrew. On this detail alone we simply cannot justify a Moses, Jesus, or Tubman typology. For the same reason, it would be shoddy argumentation to point to Jon Snow's resurrection and immediately call him a Jesus type. One event—however significant—in the life a character does not a typology make.

	Moses	Jesus	Jon	Daenerys
spirited away as a baby to escape a murderous king	placed in a basket and sent downriver	taken to Egypt for refuge	taken to Winter-fell and given an alias	taken to Essos
brought up by a surrogate guardian	Pharaoh's daughter	Joseph	Ned Stark	Viserys
saviors of entire people groups	led Hebrew slaves out of Egypt	died as a "ransom for many"	allowed Free Folk to settle south of the Wall	"breaker of chains" for multiple groups
associated with a new social order	the Ten Commandments	the Sermon on the Mount	integration of Wildlings and Night's Watch	aims to "break the wheel" of tyranny
resurrected	--	via Easter event	via Melisandre	via (symbolically) rising from Drogo's pyre

This chart is not an attempt to show that Jon is a Jesus-type or that Dany is a Moses-type. It only shows that the stories of these characters are broadly messianic. And if so, we gain fuel for theorizing an outcome for the Iron Throne.

Simply put, neither Jon nor Dany make sense as benevolent dictators. Because they are messianic types, the logical outcomes of their stories are as government reformers.

Perhaps the messiah-type will pass down a new governing charter only to die just before reaching the promised land (à la Moses). Or perhaps the messiah will be crushed by the wheel of tyranny (à la Jesus). In either case, if there is a messiah in Martin's world, the power of the Iron Throne will be significantly diminished in favor of a new world order.

In Jon's case, his time with the Free Folk beyond the Wall had a profound impact on him. The Free Folk—while lapsing into anarchy at times—exemplified a step toward a democratically elected leader. They do not kneel to tyrants. Jon becomes so sympathetic toward the Free Folk that he begins to act and think like them; so much so that he is accused of being a traitor. This is an important plotline once Jon returns to the Night's Watch (a group that also elects its leader). His affection for the "Wildlings" changes the policies of the group dramatically. After Jon is elected to be Lord Commander of the Night's Watch, he reforms the order to include the Free Folk. His message of inclusion draws the ire of his brothers, and he is murdered for it. It is simply not in Jon's character to rule as the kings before him have ruled. And, of course, he mirrors the same stubborn commitment to his ideals that we previously saw in Ned Stark. If Jon Snow ends up on the Iron Throne, it stands to reason that his reformer tendencies and messianic patterns will impact his view of governance.

In Dany's case, her experience of being sold (by marriage) like a slave has impacted her political motives and will continue to do so. She saw the way that Dothraki men abused the women of Lhazar and attempted to reform it. She saw the treatment of the Unsullied as a slave army and attempted to reform it. In liberating the slaves of Yunkai and Meereen, she names herself "Breaker of Chains." Indeed, Dany is so motivated to create a world without slaves that she lingers in Essos longer than anyone expects (annoying councilors and readers alike). She quite literally has a messiah complex. This key characteristic is at the heart of her desire to "break the wheel" of oppression in the Seven Kingdoms.

Breaking the Wheel:
Martin's Messiahs

AT THIS POINT we're going to make a fairly large assumption in deciding to treat Jon and Danny as one Messianic Unit. In our defense, after the events of season 7, it seems fair to assume that Jon and Dany will be united in purpose, and for them to continue to play their messianic role, they'll have to make lasting changes to the politics and culture of Westeros. Put another way, one or both of our lovebirds will attempt to "break the wheel"—even if said wheel kills him/her/them. Arguably, something like this already happened to Jon as a consequence of his reformation of Night's Watch policy. For the sake of this exploration, we're going to assume that Jon and Dany will be working toward like purposes.

It will be important to decide what we think Dany means when she says that she intends to "break the wheel." One thing to note is that she doesn't exempt the Targaryen dynasty from her intentions to break the wheel, listing them among the Lannisters, Starks, Tyrells, and the other "spokes on the wheel . . . crushing those on the ground" (S06E10, "The Winds of Winter"). This is evidence that Daenerys doesn't believe that just removing the usurpers and pretenders to the throne will be enough.

❧ *Excursus: Dual Messiahs at the Dead Sea* ❧

Modern groupthink about "the Messiah" is shaped by the Christian version of this concept. Centuries of preaching, European art, Sunday school, and South Park have conditioned us to associate "the Messiah" with "the Christ."[109]

109. Messiah is a Hebrew term that literally means "anointed one." In this case, it has the sense of a leader who has been ritually anointed with oil. The term "Christos" is the Greek translation of the word.

But this was not always so. Before Jesus laced up his sandals and challenged all comers to a Galilean dance-off, Jewish ideas about messiahs varied. Take, for example, the priestly group that collected the Dead Sea Scrolls (ca. 200 BCE–200 CE).[110]

The Dead Sea Scrolls showcase some of these hopes. Specifically, this group hoped for at least *two* messiahs. They called the first the "Messiah of Israel." This guy was supposed to be a righteous king. They called the second the "Messiah of Aaron." This guy was supposed to be the new high priest.[111] This dynamic duo was supposed to lead Israel into a ritually pure condition. And, in their opinion, the priestly messiah was more important than the royal messiah.

110. This group—often called the Essenes—was once prominent among Jerusalem elites. But as political regimes changed in the city *(stupid Romans!)* the true priests were removed from the Jerusalem temple and forced into the wilderness near the Dead Sea (at least, this is *their* version of the story). This group believed themselves to be the one and only true priesthood, as opposed to those usurpers in Herod's temple. As is often the case, when usurpers are in charge, the ousted party begins to hope for a new golden age.

111. Some scholars think that the Dead Sea community actually expected three messiahs. The third was a prophetic messiah.

Looking into her own family's legacy may well be enough to teach her that the Targaryens have a long history of wheeling and dealing (and crushing). Aegon the Conqueror[112] united most of Westeros[113] under his rule by his force of will and the company of very large, very powerful dragons. By all accounts, the realm prospered from the unification and his rule was largely peaceful and just after, you know, all the conquering.

Then he died of a stroke at sixty-four and his son Aenys suffered constant war and rebellion as Westeros tried to return to their old Seven Kingdom ways. He died just five years after taking the throne, and his half-brother Maegor succeeded him. Maegor was dubbed "the Cruel," and the realm was plunged into bloodshed and tyranny. Succeeding Maegor was Jaehaerys, known as "the Wise," who presided over fifty years of peace and prosperity. He was followed by his son, Viserys, who saw divisions within the Targaryen household deepen, and—despite possessing

112. The following Targaryen history lesson is courtesy *The World of Ice & Fire,* "The Targaryen Kings."

113. Except Dorne. There is a reason they still get to style themselves as Prince and Princess, and their house words are "Unbent. Unbowed. Unbroken."

the wealth and goodwill his father's rule brought—proved ineffective in bringing the sub-factions together. And so his son Aegon II inherited a civil war that became known as "The Dance of Dragons," which, aside from spilling a lot of Targaryen blood, also squandered their greatest weapons: the dragons.

Onward the wheel spun: good king, bad king, "meh" king. Sometimes the realm prospered, sometimes it bled.[114] Dany has to know that no matter how good a queen she may make, or how wise and even-tempered a King Jon "Aegon VI" Snow would be, they'd be just another spoke in the wheel. A solid one to be sure, but even Tyrion, the Hand of the Queen, ponders, "After you break the wheel, how do we make sure it stays broken?" (S07E06, "Beyond the Wall").

Moreover, we know this history, as well; it has been much-lamented by figures we like and respect in the canon, such as Tyrion and Varys. Having a "good" king or queen sit the Iron Throne would feel like a regression back to some sort of political mean. Martin knows it, too. In an interview where he discusses his "quibbles" with Tolkien, he says, *Lord of the Rings had a very medieval philosophy: that if the king was a good man, the land would prosper. We look at real history and it's not that simple. Tolkien can say that Aragorn became king and reigned for a hundred years, and he was wise and good. But Tolkien doesn't ask the question: What was Aragorn's tax policy? Did he maintain a standing army? What did he do in times of flood and famine? And what about all these orcs?*[115]

It seems that Martin himself at least plans to answer these types of wonkish political and economic questions. That means it is possible to examine the state of his world and draw conclusions about what he might intend. Many

114. While we're on the subject of the Messiah, those of us who paid attention in our synagogues and Bible schools might remember the kings of ancient Israel and Judah as depicted in the books of Kings following a similar pattern. This is par for the course with monarchies. We bring up this particular pattern because times of turmoil usually lead to a common hope for a future leader that will embody the best attributes of the glory days. Such a hope is fertile ground for messianic expectation.

115. George R. R. Martin, interview by Mikal Gilmore, May 8, 2014, issue of *Rolling Stone.*

fans over the years have put their heads together and have tried to piece together a solution to the Song's central mystery: Who will sit the Iron Throne when all has been said and done? But some fans have wondered if we're even asking the right question.

HISTORICAL BACKDROP: ATHENIAN DEMOCRACY

MEDIEVAL EUROPE WAS—IN many ways—the cultural aftermath of the Roman Empire. The reality of the so-called "Roman Republic" was long gone, and various forms of imperial rule brought various degrees of prosperity to regions like Britannia. Before the Magna Carta, the monarch's rule was absolute and unquestioned. After its impact in 1215, certain lords and barons began the long, slow process of diminishing the king's power.

It would take centuries, however, before these various tax, inheritance, and judicial laws could be called a "democracy," in the Greek sense of that word. So if we look only to medieval Europe, we might conclude—like fools!— that democracy is a modern concept. But, wise reader, you are no fool. The idea of democracy was well known (even if seldom practiced) long before. How long? Forget Great Britain and forget Rome! Rather, consider the culture that Rome copied: Hellenic Antiquity. Specifically, the city-state of Athens boasted a radical democracy in the fifth century BCE.

In its golden years, the citizens of Athens voted (i.e., direct democracy) on everything from leaders to boat maintenance. The government was divided into three branches: the Assembly, the Council of Five Hundred, and the People's Court. *In your face, Judge Wapner!* But even in its infancy (ca. 7th c.), Athens attempted to downgrade the king's power with the shared governance of three rulers: Aristotle wrote that the king became just one of three "Archons" who ruled the city-state.

So even before every citizen had a voice and vote, the Athenian government began to limit the powers of the king. This is what Aristotle would call an oligarchy.[116] It is noteworthy that Martin's portrait of Volantis copies this three-headed ruler model. Martin even borrows the concept of one-year terms from Athenian proto-democracy. While it would be another two hundred-plus years before Athens could truly claim to be a direct democracy, this separation of powers marks an important step in the process. In the same way, if Dany hopes to break the wheel of tyranny, she will need to establish the first steps of a democratic momentum that outlives her.

FAN THEORY FUN: A DREAM OF DEMOCRACY[117]

IN REAL LIFE, we know that under feudalism the monarchs were forced to give their powers over slowly to the powerful lords, who in turn were forced to slowly give power to the people(s) themselves. Their alternative was to be overthrown in violent revolutions and be replaced by some version of a republic. While some may scoff at the idea of democracy ascending in Westeros, a close reading and viewing will reveal signs that the winds of winter might blow some real change in that direction. To be clear, we're not suggesting Dany or Jon will be instituting any sort of "one person, one vote" policy or convening a parliament to house both lords and smallfolk. We are suggesting that Martin's dream of spring will include steps that undermine the consolidated power of the Iron Throne.

116. In his *Politics*, Aristotle goes into great deal about the different kinds of democracy—i.e., not every democracy is a pure (one citizen, one vote) democracy.

117. As far as we can tell, the first to put forth the idea of *A Song of Ice and Fire* ending with a decidedly democratic bent is a person by the name of Hoopdescoop on A Forum of Ice and Fire (fan forum), in a post entitled "Is Democracy the Ultimate Ending for Westeros," on May 7, 2012.

First, we have the many institutions in the world that already have democratic fundamentals. For example, the Night's Watch, which is a true representative democracy, lest one conclude that Westeros just can't handle such a thing. *Every* brother of the Watch gets a vote, and anyone can be nominated. Not only can every brother vote—from the First Ranger down to the lowest-born steward cleaning out stables and latrines—but anyone can potentially rise to the station of Lord Commander. This election process is recognizably democratic: the candidates give speeches, lobby their fellow brothers for support, and hold free and fair elections. Not for nothing, but one of our messiahs came up in this organization, and despite his background as bastard became Lord Commander. Jon may well see the virtue of this organizational structure. Indeed, his time beyond the Wall only reinforced his egalitarian leanings.

The Iron Islanders have another traditional system for electing a king that they've recently resurrected: the kingsmoot. The Ironborn may be the least civil society in Westeros, but they sure know how to moot. All longboat captains gather on Nagga's Hill on Old Wyk. Any may make a bid for the Driftwood Crown. They then make a speech detailing their accomplishments and fitness for rule, outline their policies for the Ironborn, and then demonstrate their value by distributing a generous share of their personal fortune. The king is then chosen by a simple majority vote (*World*, "Driftwood Crowns"; *Feast*, "The Drowned Man").

Then we have the Valyrian Freehold. Before the Doom of Valyria turned the Valyrian peninsula into the Smoking Sea, the Freehold became the largest and most advanced empire in the known world. On paper, all free-born landholders had an equal say in the affairs of state. While a nice concept, in practice the most wealthy and powerful families ran roughshod over the less wealthy and powerful, leading to a de facto oligarchy. But still, it was democratic in structure and ideology (*World,* "The Rise of Valyria"). Again, not for nothing, our other messiah is from this stock and may well romanticize the notion when talking about breaking the wheel.

Finally, we turn to Volantis, the oldest of the Free Cities. Volantis is ruled by the Triarchs, three figures who are elected to rule the city jointly. They serve for single-year terms, but have no set term limits. This democracy is snobbier than most, requiring every man and woman who votes and who hopes to hold office to be able to trace their bloodlines back to the time of the Valyrian Freehold. Interestingly, Volantis has two political parties: the "elephants" (who tend to be merchants and bankers, favoring trade, and alliances) and the "tigers" (who tend to be aristocrats and warriors, favoring conquest and domination). Their elections are ten-day affairs, full of speeches and performances. These include elephants carrying billboards emblazoned with political slogans and candidate names, as well as plenty of bribery, corruption, and twisting of arms (*World,* "The Free Cities: Volantis").

In sum, Martin's worldbuilding includes various forms of democracy, even if corrupt or thinly veiled fronts for other kinds of government. But the objection that democratic ideals are anachronistic or alien to Martin's world is flatly incorrect. The people who speak such nonsense are bad people who probably wash their feet in the kitchen sink (but we forgive them; they weren't properly introduced to hygiene). In fact, Martin is playing with proto-democracy on multiple levels and in various ways. In and of itself, this is not proof that the Seven Kingdoms will adopt some sort of representative government. But it remains a live possibility, especially if the character arcs of Jon and Dany keep bending in this direction. Of course, if they want to keep playing super-savior-power-couple, they will have to overcome a few forces that will resist the winds of progress.

BIRD'S-EYE VIEW: SMALLFOLK ECONOMICS

EARLIER IN THIS chapter, we included a quotation from Martin questioning Aragorn's tax, welfare, and foreign policies. Martin is playing with some of the questions that Aristotle and Demosthenes tried to answer in their critique of the Athenian democracy. Moreover, he has consciously given us a messianic figure in Dany, who wants to reinvent the usual patterns of government. Dany, as we have seen, descends from a culture (like the Greeks) that was once democratic. Not only does she care about "breaking the wheel," she is specifically interested in the well-being of the smallfolk, women, and former slaves. These all bring economic concerns to the table, as Martin has forecasted.

In Westeros, the smallfolk are truly a pitiable lot. They're expendable, illiterate, their lives often brutish and short. In the books and the series, they have borne the brunt of the War of the Five Kings. The folk who evaded death in the war now face a winter with no harvest, and are far more likely to die than survive the cold weather, to say nothing of the upcoming war against the White Walkers.

We get a grim confirmation of this fact when the Hound has occasion to revisit a farmer whom he robbed some time ago (S07E01, "Dragonstone"). He finds the man and his daughter, dead and frozen in their croft. When societies reach this kind of crisis, violent uprisings are just around the corner. Moreover, the promise of food and security tend to overcome traditional attachments to a particular liege lord or ruling class. In the case of Westeros, those keeping the "King's peace" are among the most dangerous dudes on the kingsroad. If a new ruler were to establish herself—let's imagine one with two or three dragons—with enough resources to feed and protect the smallfolk, they would care much less about ideology and much more about bread.

Eventually, the wars and winter of the Baratheon period will be over. Someone will have to work the fields, tend the flocks, and shovel stables. The demand for labor will far outstrip the supply, giving the smallfolk incentive to move where lords potentially offer better pay and living conditions. As a by-product, old alliances and old traditions will weaken as the balance of power shifts.

In a related point, if Westeros has a labor shortage, this will make immigration from Essos very attractive. These immigrants will bring new cultures, foods, politics, and other ideas from the Free Cities. This could stimulate changing attitudes toward merchant classes that are already very powerful in Essos, such as the Iron Bank of Braavos. Smallfolk and immigrants with coin in the pocket they can use to better themselves may well lead to the rise of a middle class. Skilled tradesmen such as armorers, tanners, masons, and tailors will enjoy this newfound market for their products and skills, making their guilds more powerful.

Other frequently overlooked members of society, such as bastards and women, stand to improve their lot for many of the same reasons. With so many great and noble houses utterly decimated (if not destroyed), inheritances and titles will have to go to somebody, and in some cases these will have to be daughters and illegitimate sons. Empowering these traditionally oppressed classes could further move the trend toward tolerance and fair representation.

The destruction of the Wall, and reconciling the Free Folk tribes back into the "realms of men" by Jon Snow, could lead to an integration of Westerosi and Free Folk cultures. Those from the True North are famous for refusing to kneel, and have relatively egalitarian views (e.g., the social status of women and bastards).

The collapse of a strong central government might, like the death of Aegon the Conqueror, have a lot of lords dreaming of the days of the Seven Kingdoms again. If the North wants their King in the North, and the Dornish want to go back to the Unbent, Unbowed, Unbroken days, who is to stop them? It's easy to imagine how the Iron Throne might well accept some form of power limitations. For what it's worth, Dany promises something along these lines to the Ironborn (show only; S06E09, "Battle of the Bastards"). Perhaps the winner of the Game of Thrones will allow some form of power-sharing with the nobility in order to stave off an all-out rebellion of the few powerful houses that will be left. It's interesting that similar conditions led to the Magna Carta, one of the first documents to check the "God-given" power of the king of England.

If Dany manages to survive the upcoming war to see the dream of spring, there is also the issue of Daenerys being barren. This fact is disputed by many, and remains ambiguous in the text. Regardless, as of season 7 of *Game of Thrones,* Dany herself believes she is barren. Tyrion points out the difficulty and danger of starting a dynasty without heirs.

Again, we can't say for sure what form of democracy Westeros might take. We do observe, however, that the political, economic, and plot forces seem ripe for the lords and ladies of the realm to take back some of their power.

Once they do, how far behind can the smallfolk be? Both Dany and Jon have democratic traditions in their past. Both were once outcasts and pariahs but made the most of their luck and skills to rise to the tops of their respective societies. Both are skeptical of supreme power, and have seen firsthand the corruption and abuse that can arise from it. Both are already accomplished saviors of their respective peoples and are faced with the question: *How can you keep a society secure and free forever?*

Missandei once explained to Jon and Ser Davos the essential strength of Daenerys' claim to the throne. "We believe in her. She's not our queen because she's the daughter of some king we never knew. She's the queen we *chose*" (S07E04, "The Spoils of War").

It worked before. Why not again?

Volume 1 Wrap
THE ALMIGHTY STORY

MARTIN'S WORLD IS A PRECARIOUS PLACE. THE SHADOW of death hangs over every character, regardless of how well loved. Moreover, "doing the right thing" might kill or king you (being kinged can hasten your demise, too). *A Game of Thrones* begins with the beheading of a man who has acted contrary to his duty. This book ends with the beheading of a man who has done his duty to the best of his ability. Essentially, this is a world of chaos—the very thing that religion is supposed to stave off.

When asked about liquidating his characters, Martin explained, "It's a little like killing a part of yourself or smothering one of your children, but sometimes it has to be done for the almighty god of the story."[118]

In a sense, the Almighty Story is the true monotheistic God of Westeros. The followers of R'hllor may claim that the "Lord of Light" is the only god. But they also believe in the Great Other. Similarly, the Greyjoys are devoted to the Drowned God. But this deity is at war with the Storm God in Ironborn mythology. The Lhazareen Great Shepherd is indeed monotheistic, but represents a religion in Essos (not Westeros).

We do, however, meet Braavosi characters in Westeros. Both Jaqen H'ghar and Syrio Forel hail from Braavos and become guides for Arya. Arya learns that the "Many-Faced God"—the only true god—is the god of death. If so, this in-world god functions very much like Martin's meta-world God. It is the Almighty Story that organizes all fates and fatalities.

118. Amy Lee, "'Game of Thrones' Author George R. R. Martin Answers Fans' Questions Live," *Huffington Post*, July 28, 2011.

But Braavosi universalism and Arya are topics for volume 2. The next volume will also include deep dives into Ironborn mythology, Dothraki bro-culture, and the dragon cult. Until then, *valar morghulis.*

Can't wait to know what happens next
 with the religions of Westeros and beyond?

Neither can we!
But we are delighted to present you
with this special preview from

Gods of Thrones, volume 2
(it won't take a decade to write, we promise)

This excerpt is from our chapter
"Here Be Dragons"

SONS OF DRAGONS

ARTIN'S INTEREST IN dragons is shaped in large part by European legends. But there are a few unmistakable parallels to Chinese dragon mythology, too.[1] Chinese dragon mythology probably grows out of alligator lore. The Chinese logogram *T'o* is sometimes interpreted as "alligator" and sometimes as "earth dragon."[2] This association is key to understanding their place in mythology and religion. In the Tang, Qing, and Han dynasties, dragons were treated as rain gods that governed the weather. They were thought to reside below water (being of the same family as alligators). In the work of Confucius, dragons tend to show up prior to or just after rainfall.

During times of drought, farmers preformed rituals to get the attention of sleeping dragons. Some of these rituals—like submerging a tiger skull in the river—were supposed to scare the beasts out of the water and into the sky. According to tradition, the simple act of a dragon moving from water to sky would bring rainfall. Dragons were sort of like evaporation before modern science had a better word for it. Other rituals—like ritually beating a small lizard to death with bamboo—would get the dragon's attention in the same way a sacrificial offering was meant to work. In northern China, regular prayer was performed to dragons before the rainy season to ensure good crops.

The first ritual demonstrates the place that dragons and tigers occupied in mythology. The tiger symbolized drought while the dragon symbolized rain. From this yin (dragons) and yang (tigers) perspective, dragons were necessary and positive. These are not the fell beasts

1. Most of this section is owed to John Thorbjarnarson and Xiaoming Wang, *The Chinese Alligator: Ecology, Behavior, Conservation, and Culture* (Baltimore: Johns Hopkins University Press, 2010).

2. Thorbjarnarson and Wang, *Alligator*, 61. *T'o* is notoriously difficult to translate. It seems to apply to any number of large water lizards in ancient texts.

of European lore or the sociopathic greed-monsters of Inkling imagination; rather dragons are rain deities, bringing fortune with them. It is important to keep in mind that such deities were not—like Western minds associate with divinity—all-knowing or all-powerful. Dragons are divine in the sense that they are mythological beasts with powers that can sometimes be manipulated by humans. Only it doesn't always go well for the humans.

Chinese emperors have a long history of using dragons as sigils. In the same way that the dragon is able to ascend from water to heaven, the emperor also ascends to heaven. The association was meant to reinforce the great power of royalty: they had godlike powers. Bang Liu (ca. 2nd c. BCE) was called the dragon's "Seed," meaning that his father was a literal dragon. As the first emperor of the Western Han Dynasty, Bang Liu's legend cemented the ruling class as sons of dragons (i.e., they were sons of the gods comparable to Egyptian pharaohs).

This backdrop shows a few obvious parallels to Targaryen mythos and a few obvious differences. The most glaring difference is that Martin's dragons are fire-breathing, warmongering, gluttons. They may represent fortune (for those who can't point them in the right direction and say *dracarys*) but they also represent mass-destruction. They're not, in other words, like rainfall in a drought (which benefits everyone). So in this way, Martin's dragons are decidedly influenced by European legend. Also, Martin's dragons (most of them, anyway) don't sleep under water or get spooked by tiger skulls. That said, the parallels are too intriguing to dismiss.

1. The Targaryens use dragons as their sigils.

2. Dragons are associated with the Old Valyrian gods (e.g., Balerion, Meraxes, Vhagar, and Syrax are all dragons named after gods).

3. The Targaryens believe themselves to be related by blood to dragons.

4. Daenerys (a.k.a. "Stormborn") is born during a famously rainy night.

Could it be that Martin was influenced in some way by Chinese dragon mythology?[3] And if so, consider this: the main benefit of Chinese dragons is to bring positive balance to the weather; could it be that Martin's dragons are meant to restore balance to the imbalanced seasons of Westeros?[4] Maybe the Westerosi farmers who don't get marshmallowed by Dany will benefit from spring showers after the Others are defeated.

CHARACTER STUDY: TYRION

L OOK, WE DON'T know if Tyrion is a secret Targaryen. In volume 1, we gave a few good reasons to consider this theory. But it must remain a theory. What is clear—what we will argue with great argumentative arguing—is that Martin has something big planned for Tyrion. Consider the evidence:

1. (1) Early in the story, Tyrion is foreshadowed as a *big deal*—maybe in the sense of royalty, but at least in the sense of Burgundy. This is first foreshadowed after his famous exchange with . . .

Tyrion and company will return in volume 2.

Acknowledgments

3. Probably.

4. Possibly.

175

Acknowledgments

A PSEUDO-ACADEMIC BOOK ABOUT FAKE RELIGIONS doesn't get written without a lot of pretend hard work. It also requires a great deal of real-life help. We are grateful to our artist, Chase Stone, who—as you can see—is talented beyond measure. We are also grateful to Steve Gentile who went above and beyond our expectations with the typesetting and overall design, and to Erika Stokes who adapted the material into the ebook format. Joshua Paul Smith, Karl Coppock, and Sarah Le Donne were our stellar copyeditors. Any remaining errors were surely added to the manuscript by A.Ron and Anthony after their keen eyes were done editing.

This book would not be possible without the fine people who supported our Kickstarter campaign. That there is such optimism in the world for creative endeavors is incredibly humbling. Our sincere gratitude to all who contributed and special thanks to the names listed in the final pages of this book.

GRATITUDE FROM A.RON:

Thanks go, in no particular order, to my co-author, Anthony, for approaching me with the idea for this book, and in general for being such a thoughtful, intelligent, and patient guy. My participation in this book is entirely due to his enthusiasm and persistence.

To my co-host Jim for allowing me to devote my time and attention to this project, which necessarily took time away from my responsibilities to our podcasting empire.

What an amazing thing we've built together! I'm so glad to be your friend.

To my wife Cecily, for her love, support, encouragement, and feedback. For a long time now, you've been my biggest fan, and I hope I bring half as much joy to your life as you bring to mine.

To my son Jack, for giving me a wondrous tour through fatherhood. I can't wait to see the man you will become! To my father for teaching me so much, and bestowing upon me your strength, intellectual curiosity and incredible resourcefulness. Why couldn't I get your hairline?! To my sister for being a real and genuine pain in my ass right up until the day I looked around and saw that you had somehow became one of the strongest women I know. To the men I call brother: Daniel, Josh, Matt, and Nick, for all of the laughs, tears, and council. Shout out to the "J" conspiracy for adopting a stray into their pack. To my actual brother. It's not too late, kid. I miss you. To my grandfather, who was in real life the man John Wayne played in the movies. You were a real badass, grandpa. But to our great loss, valar morghulis.

Finally, to the incredible people that make up the Bald Move community, for giving me a life I would never have dared to dream of, literally growing up in the cornfields of Indiana. Hell, you all even financed the publishing of this book! I'll forever be grateful to be a part of such a warm, funny, and smart collection of humanity.

GRATITUDE FROM ANTHONY:

I would like to thank the following people for reading over portions of this book and offering constructive feedback: Chad Carmichael, Stephanie Barbé Hammer, Andrew Knapp, Tara LeDonne Jenkins, and Nathan Strong.

I'm also indebted to my children, Nessa Le Donne and Beren Le Donne, who share my love of dragons, mythology, and words. Splendiferous thanks goes to my wife, Sarah, who makes me a better writer and a better person.

Hey, A.Ron and Jim, thanks for creating this community and for bringing joy to so many people. My deepest gratitude to Mr. Hubbard who made this project fun.

A WORD TO R. R.

We both want to thank George Martin for being the masterful storyteller that he is. If, in these pages, we aim too often for the chinks in his armor, it is because his conquest of the fantasy-literature world is unassailable. George, as you well know, sitting the throne of your own creation makes you powerful beyond measure and vulnerable only to the songs of court jesters. Our critical comments are little more than doting lyrics from Patchface and Moon Boy.

A.Ron and Anthony would also like to acknowledge the people that supported the Kickstarter campaign that funded the production of this book. In a very literal sense, this book would not be possible without the following incredibly supportive and generous individuals. . .

Gold Dragon Tier

Adam Edrington ❀ Ann Merin ❀ Ashley Nelani Paulus

Brenna Sardar ❀ Bryan Hayward Stell ❀ Caren Pelletier

Carma A. Clark ❀ Catherine ❀ Chris Churchman

Colleen Gonzalez ❀ Dani Lipari-Mareth

Danielle Mathieson ❀ David "Kamish" Stern ❀ David Aguiar

Gregory Senger ❀ Janice O'Brien ❀ Jarrod Harleman ❀ Jenni Tahmassebi ❀ Jennie L. Rexer, PhD ❀ Jessi Pitt

Jim Quinn ❀ Joel Tacorda ❀ Kay Bonikowsky

Kilted Viking ❀ Kimmmy Lucas ❀ Kirk and Leila S

Kris Isham ❀ KWQ ❀ Lady Jillian Walsh

Laura E. Luethe ❀ Martin Monarrez

Maximus Otto of House Forster ❀ Michael Johnston

Mike McCorkle ❀ ML Fantacone ❀ Nicholas Blau

Nikki Carrow ❀ Patrick Barnhart ❀ Richard Frette

Richard Hamm ❀ Richard Kerkhof ❀ Ser Andrew Hoover

Shawn ❀ Sir Kory of House Boogerlip ❀ Steven Sprague

Tim Satterlee ❀ Tim Wolffgang Rasmussen

Tony "letrbuck" Busby ❀ Tyler Shumway

Valerie "Best Little Sister Ever" Bedel

William Blake ❀ xulsolar22

Silver Stag Tier

A.K. Cuttner ✳ Alex M Capasso ✳ Alexandria Leuzzi ✳

Andrew Kasprisin ✳ Andrew McLeod Maggard ✳ Ashley Wagner

Audrey Heathman ✳ Austin Egloff ✳ Barksdale Hortenstine, Jr.

Blake Bequette ✳ Brad Ward ✳ Brian Ward ✳ c:\ ✳ Carmelita Valdez McKoy

✳ Cecelia Gray ✳ Cecily ✳ Chase R.R. Mulberry

Chelsea Tyus ✳ Chris Mullan ✳ Chris Webber ✳ Christine Brown

Christine Shrum ✳ Christopher Carter ✳ Chuck James

Cody Harris ✳ Craig Gutteridge ✳ Dan Burns & Amanda Nicholson

Dave Milne ✳ David K. ✳ Dean M. Welsh ✳ Doshy Ellison

Drew Davis ✳ Dustin Mott ✳ Dylan Blank ✳ Dylan P. Angeline

Eddie & Amy Cook ✳ Eric from Minneapolis ✳ Eric Harzer

Erica Scharbach ✳ Erin C. Badillo ✳ Exilein ✳ Georgia Leigh

Graham Conroy ✳ Gregory Rasp ✳ House McGee ✳ Ivonne Reyna

J. Ayala ✳ Jacob Bryant ✳ Jake Ollanketo ✳ Jamie E. Massaro

Jamie H. ✳ Jared from KC ✳ Jasneet Mander ✳ Jeanette Volintine

Jeremy N. ✳ Jernious Pennyford

Joanna -"The Winged Wolf" De Arman ✳ Joel Johnson

Joffrey Engelman ✳ Jon Tinter ✳ Jord ✳ Jordan Ellena

Jordan Nazario ✳ Josh K. ✳ Joshua & Katelyn Triplette

Joshua Wilson, 297th of his name ✳ JSB ✳ jsl ✳ Julien

Justin Freiberg ✳ Kate B. F. ✳ Kevin O'Donnell ✳ Kevin P. Cattani

Kim Cook ✳ Kimberly L. ✳ Kody Clark ✳ Kyle L. Long

Lady Amanda, Mother of Cats and Dragons and defender of Boston

Laura Hamilton ✳ Lee G. Madden ✳ Levi & Liz ✳ Lisa K. G.

Lord Franz Stein Master of Complaints ✳ Lucas From Milwaukee

Lucy Feekins ✳ Luke A. Sinden ✳ M. Kalin-Casey

Maester Beverly Lewis ✳ Marci McClenon ✳ Margaret Dwyer

Marjorie Weyers ✳ Mark Hahn ✳ Mark P (counterpoint)

Mathew K Martinez ✳ Maura Ruth Hashman ✳ Meagan Ellis

Meaghan Fallano ✳ Michael ✳ Michael Choi ✳ Michael James

Mike Hazen ✳ Nate Augustine ✳ Nathan Van Aken ✳ Nellie Cho

Nick Z ✳ Nickolas J. Berra ✳ Nicole Whatley ✳ Olivia Deck

Patrick O'Brien ✳ Paul T. ✳ Peggy "Regular Girl" Boynton

Rachel Harrison ✳ Rev. Jeremy D. Smith ✳ Rhys Davey

Rich Glinka ✳ Robert N Costa ✳ Roger Dotsey ✳ Rosa T.

SBench2 ✳ Sean Patrick Dennison ✳ Seth Edwards

Shaun Gresham ✳ Stephen M. Reynolds ✳ Steve Heineman

Steve Lionetti ✳ Steven Duran ✳ Thomas S. Melanson

Tiffiny Mansouri ✳ Tim Grable ✳ Tom de Planque

Trevor A. Ramirez ✳ Tyler Hardy ✳ Vic Kowalski ✳ Zach Ziemke

Copper Penny Tier

Adele Beegle ∿ Alec Jenkins ∿ Alexa Sonderman ∿ alina_mac ∿ Amy Wagner
Andres Blanco ∿ Anthony Fassano ∿ Anthony Sosa ∿ Caleb Thrower ∿ Casey Caldwell
Cherri Wright ∿ Chris "Flukes" Chambers ∿ Christy Heyl ∿ Cory Peace
Damien Armstrong ∿ Dan Schnock ∿ Destonie ∿ Doctor Nick ∿ Elizabeth Adams
Elizabeth Oxer ∿ Garett "gnarzz" Guenot ∿ Georgio "Bald Targaryen" Vuolde
Gina Michaelson ∿ Heather J. ∿ Heather Malin ∿ Hero James ∿ Isabel M. ∿ Jaimie Teekell
James H Park ∿ James Morris Anderson ∿ Jenni Wright ∿ Jennifer Rodriguez ∿ Jenny Olson
Kevin C. ∿ Kristina Corona ∿ Lorien Bree Leonard-Walonen ∿ Makenzie F.
Maureen Carroll ∿ MBMom ∿ Meghan Flanigan ∿ Melody H. ∿ Michael W Murphy
Michelle Tuel ∿ Mike Condo ∿ Nancy Howell ∿ Nichole H. ∿ Nick Bonds ∿ Nick Scarci
Nicole Hackney ∿ Nicole Klope ∿ Noelle Joseph ∿ Pablo Trejo ∿ Patrick Walsh
Rachel H. ∿ Renée Margaux ∿ Robert K. Crawford ∿ Ronida Oum ∿ Sarah Larsen
Sean F. Dooley ∿ Sharon Van Der Werk ∿ Stacie Calabrese ∿ Stan Lindesmith
Steve Gentile ∿ Steve Savaille ∿ thamesgirl ∿ Tom Norgate ∿ Tom_G in WV
Tracee M. Jordan ∿ Zan Shadbolt